SIMPLE CHESS

SIMPLE CHESS
NEW ALGEBRAIC EDITION

Michael Stean

Edited and translated into algebraic notation by
Fred Wilson

DOVER PUBLICATIONS
Garden City, New York

Bibliographical Note

This Dover edition, first published in 2002, is a new algebraic edition of the work first published in descriptive notation by Faber & Faber, London, in 1978.
Fred Wilson translated the original 1978 text into algebraic notation for this edition. The present edition was designed and formatted by Jill Meadows.

Library of Congress Cataloging-in-Publication Data

Stean, Michael.
  Simple chess / Michael Stean.—New algebraic ed. / edited and translated into algebraic notation by Fred Wilson.
      p. cm.
  Previous ed.: London : Faber & Faber, 1978.
  ISBN-13: 978-0-486-42420-0
  ISBN-10: 0-486-42420-0
    1. Chess. I. Wilson, Fred. II. Title.

GV1449.5 .S73 2002
794.1—dc21

2002034929

Manufactured in the United States of America
42420017   2022
www.doverpublications.com

SIMPLE CHESS

Michael Stean

Simple Chess is an introduction to chess strategy aimed primarily at those players for whom strategy in chess is an almost impenetrable mystery. By isolating the basic elements and illustrating them through a selection of master and grandmaster games, *Simple Chess* attempts to break down the mystique of chess strategy into plain, clear, easy-to-understand ideas. The book assumes only a knowledge of chess terminology from the reader.

Simple Chess is not solely a lesson in chess fundamentals, it also represents a style of chess playing which is becoming increasingly prevalent and successful throughout the world. Almost all the games in the book are illustrative of this style which involves a slow-build-up, gradually accumulating small but permanent advantages, with the concept of attack being shelved for the later stages of the game. It is indeed the spread and success of this style of play that prompted the writing of this book.

Michael Stean, born in 1953, is one of this country's outstanding younger players. In 1973 he was third in the World Junior Championship; in 1975 he became an International Master; and in 1977 he achieved the supreme accolade of a Grand Master title. Stean retired from competitive chess in 1982 and currently practices as a tax accountant.

Contents

1. Introduction

Don't be deceived by the title—chess is not a simple game—such a claim would be misleading to say the least—but that does not mean that we must bear the full brunt of its difficulty. When faced with any problem too large to cope with as a single entity, common sense tells us to break it down into smaller fragments of manageable proportions. For example, the arithmetical problem of dividing one number by another is not one that can in general be solved in one step, but primary school taught us to find the answer by a series of simple division processes (namely long division). So, how can we break down the 'problem' of playing chess?

Give two of the uninitiated a chessboard, a set of chessmen, a list of rules and a lot of time, and you may well observe the following process: the brighter of the two will quickly understand the idea of checkmate and win some games by 1. e4 2. Bc4 3. Qh5 4. Qxf7 mate. When the less observant of our brethren learns how to defend his f7 square in time, the games will grow longer and it will gradually occur to the players that the side with more pieces will generally *per se* be able to force an eventual checkmate. This is the first important 'reduction' in the problem of playing chess—the numerically superior force will win. So now our two novices will no longer look to construct direct mates, these threats are too easy to parry, but will begin to learn the tricks of the trade for winning material (forks, skewers, pins, etc.), confident that this smaller objective is sufficient. Time passes and each player becomes sufficiently competent not to shed material without reason. Now they begin to realize the importance of developing quickly and harmoniously and of castling the king into safety.

So what next? Where are their new objectives? How can the problem be further reduced? If each player is capable of quick development, castling and of not blundering any pieces away, what is there to separate the

1

two sides? This is the starting-point of *Simple Chess*. It tries to reduce the problem still further by recommending various positional goals which you can work towards, other things (i.e. material, development, security of king position) being equal. Just as our two fictitious friends discovered that the one with more pieces can expect to win if he avoids any mating traps, *Simple Chess* will provide him with some equally elementary objectives which if attained should eventually decide the game in his favor, subject to the strengthened proviso that he neither allows any mating tricks, nor loses any material *en route*.

Essentially, *Simple Chess* aims to give you some of the basic ideas for forming a long-term campaign. It also shows you how to recognize and accumulate small, sometimes almost insignificant-looking advantages which may well have little or no short-term effect, but are *permanent* features of the position. As the game progresses, the cumulative effect begins to make itself felt more and more, leading eventually to more tangible gains. This style of play is simple and economical both in its conception and execution. Combinations and attacks are shelved for their proper time and place as the culmination of an overall strategy. Given the right kind of position it is not so difficult to overwhelm the opposition with an avalanche of sacrifices. The real problem is how to obtain such positions. This is the objective of *Simple Chess*.

Undoubtedly the best way to improve your chess is by studying master and grandmaster games. For this reason I have used a selection of such games as a medium through which to put across the fundamental principles of simple chess. These games are mostly not of the type to capture the limelight of chess literature because they are too simple and unsensational, but for this very reason they are suitable for showing off clearly the basic ideas I want to convey.

As a preliminary to splitting the elements of simple chess into an array of recognizable objectives, as will occur in the ensuing chapters, I want to give you something of the flavor of what is to come in the form of three introductory games containing most of the concepts and strategies to be elaborated later on. The first is a victory by ex-World Champion Mikhail Botvinnik over the Hungarian International Master Szilagyi in Amsterdam, 1966. One of the truly great masters of strategy, Botvinnik gives a typically powerful and very instructive display. We pick up the play in diagram 1 with Botvinnik (White) to move:

1.

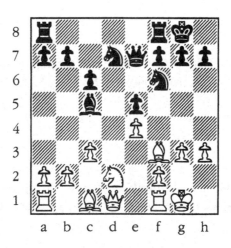

The position may at first sight seem quite good for Black. His pieces occupy good squares in the center, his king is very safe and he has a lead in development having already connected his rooks on the back rank while White is a long way from doing so. However, positionally he has problems arising from the exchange of his Queen's Bishop for a Knight. In the long run he will find difficulty in defending his White squares. We shall see what this means in more tangible terms as the game progresses.

12.   b4

A space-gaining move. The center is fixed and White

does not want to advance on the Kingside for fear of exposing his own monarch, so the logical zone for expansion is on the Queenside.

12.   ...   Bb6
13.   a4   Rfd8

Black dare not hit back with13...a5 because of 14. Ba3 followed by Nc4 or Nb3 with lots of dangerous possibilities on the a3-f8 diagonal.

14.   Qc2   Rac8

Black already finds himself lacking a good plan. A better idea has 14...Nf8 followed by Ne6 and a5 trying to get a grip on c5 or d4. Black's difficulties stem from the fact that he has no good outpost for his pieces.

15.   Be2

In contrast Botvinnik's advance has given him a nice square on c4 which he can occupy with either a Knight or a Bishop.

15.   ...   c5??

Two question marks for a move which does not actually lose any material may seem a bit harsh, but I want to emphasize the point that before 15...c5 Black merely had problems, but now he is lost.

16.   b5!

2.

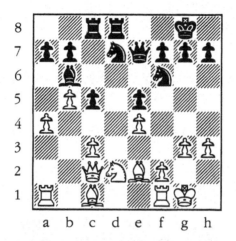

Why is Black lost? Material is equal and White hasn't got a piece beyond the second rate. The answer lies in the Pawns. White has two beautiful squares on c4 and d5, plus a mobile Pawn roller on the left flank, whereas Black's Pawns constrict his own pieces terribly, particularly the Bishop. Botvinnik now treats us to a vigorous exhibition of technical chess as he converts these advantages into a win.

16.   ...   Ne8
17.   Nc4   Nd6
18.   Bg5!

A surprise tactical shot, but its aims are positional.

18.   ...   f6

The point of the combination. Black is forced to weaken yet another White square (e6) in the heart of his position. Refusal to fall in with White's plans is even more unpalatable:

    (i) 18...Qxg5 19. Nxd6 Rb8 20. Bc4
    (ii) 18...Nf6 19 Ne3 followed by Nd5

19.	Be3	Nxc4
20.	Bxc4+	Kh8
21.	a5	Bc7
22.	Rfd1	Nf8

An exchange of Rooks will not heal Black's wounds. On the other hand, neither will anything else.

23.	Qa2	Rxd1+
24.	Rxd1	Rd8
25.	Rxd8	Bxd8
26.	a6	

Conquering yet another White square (c6) and simultaneously releasing the Queen from her defense of the a Pawn in preparation for more active service.

26.	...	b6
27.	Kg2	

White's control of the position is so great that he could inscribe his initials on the board with his King if he wanted. Being rather less self-indulgent, Botvinnik contents himself with one preparatory King move before embarking on the winning process On general principles, his King will feel safer on a White square.

27.	...	Qd7
28.	Qe2	Ng6
29.	Bb3	

At last an attack, but there's no need for any excitement. The outcome is a mere formality. With a Bishop having the mobility of a tortoise with rheumatism, Black is in no position to offer any real resistance.

29.	...	Ne7
30.	Qc4	h6

31.   Qf7!   Kh7

31...Qxb5 loses a piece to 32. Qf8+ Kh7 33. Qxd8 Qxb3 34. Qxe7.

32.   Bc4   Qd6
33.   h4

Botvinnik now weaves a mating net on the White squares.

33.   ...   Qd1
34.   Qe8

With the threat of Bf7, h5, followed by Bg6+, etc. There's no defense.

34.   ...   f5
35.   exf5   Nxf5
36.   Bg8+   Kh8
37.   Bf7+ and mates next move.

A perfect illustration of what is known as a *White square strategy*, something we will explore in more depth later on. For the moment, however, I merely want to draw your attention to the effortless simplicity with which Botvinnik established and drove home his advantage. With the possible exception of 18. Bg5!, none of his moves could in any way be described as surprising or difficult to visualize. They were all really rather obvious. So why cannot everybody play like that? Well, they can providing they recognize and understand the importance of *structure*. The most important single feature of a chess position is the activity of the pieces. This is absolutely fundamental in all phases of the game (opening, middlegame and *especially* endgame), a theme which I hope will become increasingly apparent as the book progresses. The primary constraint on piece's activity is the Pawn structure. Just as a building is constructed around a framework of iron girders, a chess game is built around an underlying structure of pawns. The difference lies in the fact that the iron framework is fixed, whereas the chessplayer has a certain amount of flexibility with his Pawns.

The job of the chessplayer must therefore be to use his skill to create a Pawn set-up which will allow his own pieces the optimum freedom and stability, while denying his opponent's similar scope. This is the problem of structure, which will be dealt with in some depth.

3.

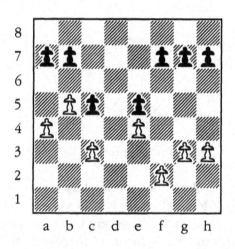

To take an example, let us go back to the position of Diagram 2 and examine it from a structural point of view. Removing the pieces from the board, but leaving the pawns, we have Diagram 3. From this we see very strong squares or *outposts* for his pieces on c4 and d5. They are strong because neither can be challenged by a Black Pawn. In contrast, Black has no outposts at all. So arithmetically speaking White had a 2-0 lead in outposts, a very healthy state of affairs. Bearing this in mind, notice the vital role played by the White Pawn on c3 guarding Black's natural outpost on d4. If White were ever to play the positionally abysmal c4? he would not only give Black his long awaited outpost, but would also smother his own c4 square, thus equalizing the outpost score to 1-1 at a stroke. Moreover the damage would be irreversible. Pawns cannot move backwards. If you inadvertently put a piece on a bad square, you can always retract it at the cost of some time (and face), but in the case of a Pawn you are lumbered with it for the rest of the game. Think twice about Pawn moves, especially in the center.

4.

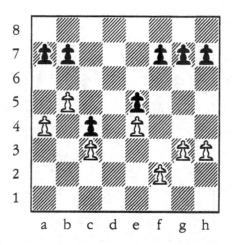

Returning to Diagram 3, is there any way for Black to improve matters, structurally speaking? Certainly. If he could advance c5-c4, the world would suddenly be a much happier place for him. Look at Diagram 4. Black now has three excellent squares c5, d3, and b3, while White has to be content with one (d5). So we see that White's c4 square is strategically the focal point of the position. Just as the outcome of a real battle may depend on control of a high point or mountain dominating the surrounding terrain, a chess game can hinge around the struggle for control of one key square. In this case it is the square c4. Do you recall Botvinnik's 15th move Be2? It may not have seemed terribly significant at the time, but in fact shows that he had already fully recognized the strategic importance of the c4 square. Clever fellows these Russians!

We now turn our attention to an even more striking demonstration of the power and importance of structure, this time given by the great master of defence Tigran Petrosian. The ninth game of his Candidates' Match with Lajos Portisch (Black) started **1. Nf3 Nf6 2. c4 g6 3. b3 Bg7 4. Bb2 c5 5. g3 d6 6. Bg2 e5 7. 0-0 Nc6 8. Nc3 0-0 9. d3 Nh5 10. Nd2 Bg4 11. a3 Bh6** reaching the position of Diagram 5.

5.

At a glance the Black pieces may seem to be menacingly poised for a Kingside attack. On the other hand a quick look at the Pawn structure reveals that White has an excellent outpost on d5, but how does that help? It certainly has no immediate value, as 12. Nd5 Nd4! 13. Bxd4 exd4 would allow Black to develop a lot of pressure on the e-file. However, the d5 square is there to stay and if it cannot be profitably utilized at present, it is nevertheless a good investment for the future. With this in mind Petrosian chose.

12.   b4!

The classical way to exploit a structural advantage in the center is with a thrust on the flank, but here accurate calculation is also required. In the event of 12...cxb4 13. axb4 Nxb4 White plays 14. Ba3! (but not 14. Bxb7 Nxd3!) with three possibilities:

(i) 14...Nxd3? 15. h3 now wins a piece.

(ii) 14...Nc6 15. N(d2) e4 winning the d pawn.

(iii) 14...a5 15. Rb1 regaining the Pawn with advantage as 15...Nxd3? still fails to 16. h3.

One might reasonably ask if it was not similar to drive away Black's Bishop with 12. h3 before playing b4 so as to avoid all the above complications based on the pin on White's e Pawn. The answer is that White does not want to make any Pawn move in front of his own King until it is *absolutely necessary*, as it merely provides Black with a ready-made target to attack. For instance, 12. h3 Bd7 13. b4 f5 and ...f4 could well be dangerous for White.

12.   ...   Nd4

Black has some very dangerous threats. Not only is 13...Bxd2 and 14...Nb3 winning the exchange in the cards, but the Tal-like sacrifice 13...Nf4! 14 gxf4 Bxf4 followed by Qh4 is also in the air.

13.   h3!

A sense of timing is the key to good defensive play. Here Petrosian accepts the weakening of his Kingside Pawns as he realizes that he can thereby completely repulse the attack.

13.   ...   Be6
14.   e3   cxb4

An anti-positional capture, but he has no alternative. After 14...Nc6 15. bxc5 dxc5 16. Nb3 Qe7 17. Na4 he simply loses a Pawn for nothing.

15.	axb4	Nc6
16.	b5	Ne7
17.	Bxb7	

Another well-calculated little venture which increases White's positional advantage still further.

17.	...	Bxh3
18.	Bxa8	Bxf1

18...Qxa8 19. Qf3 is very much the same as the game.

19.	Kxf1	Qxa8
20.	Qf3!	

A very strong move, if an equally obvious one. After 20...Qxf3 21. Nxf3 not only is Black structurally quite lost, but he has not even enough time to defend his a Pawn in view of the threatened g4 and g5 winning a piece.

20.	...	Qb8

This leads to the immediate and rather quaint loss of a piece, but there is nothing better to recommend. If you are wondering why Black is so abjectly lost, compare the Pawn structures.

21.	g4	Ng7
22.	Qf6!	

The double threat of Qxe7 and Qh4! is decisive. After the further moves **22...N(g7)f5 23. gxf5 Nxf5 24. e4 Ng7 25. Ke1 Nh5 26. Qh4 f5 27. Nd5** Black resigned.

A resoundingly decisive game to win again a World Championship contender, but Petrosian didn't have to work all that hard. His Pawns in their own quiet way did all the work for him.

In both of the preceding games, Black's structural

12

deficiency has taken the form of weak squares rather than the Pawns themselves being weak. In most cases these two effects (weak squares, weak Pawns) go hand in hand, as we shall see. For the moment, here is a game in which White uses the presence of weak Pawns in the enemy camp to tie down the Black pieces and so launch a mating attack, despite the absence of Queens.

Adorjan-Mukhin, Luhacovice, 1973

1. e4 e5 2. Nf3 Nc6 3. Bb5 a6 4. Bxc6 dxc6 5. 0-0 f6 6. d4 Bg4 7. dxe5 Qxd1 8. Rxd1 fxe5 9. Rd3 Bd6 10. Nbd2 Nf6 11. Nc4 Bxf3 12. gxf3 0-0-0

6.

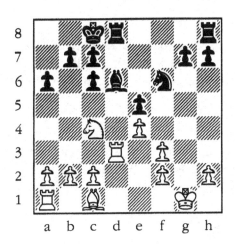

The position is tense. Black's Pawn on e5 is weak, but that is his only weakness. The doubled c Pawns are not weak, not yet at any rate. On the other hand, White's double Pawns could well become weak as they are on an open file. Moreover, Black has an outpost on f4 and if given time for Nh5 and Rhf8 could easily seize the advantage, so...

13.   Bg5

Immobilizing the Knight and threatening Rad1, which wins a Pawn.

13.   ...   b5

The only way to meet the threat of 14. Rad1. The life expectancy of Black's e Pawn would not be increased by 13...h6 14. Bh4 with Bg3 in prospect.

14.   Na5   c5
15.   c4!

Fixing the Black c5 Pawn on a vulnerable square before it marches on to the safety of c4.

15.   ...   Rdf8

He needs to unpin the Knight. 15...b4 would allow White to start an attack on the a file with 16. a3, while 15...bxc4 16. Nxc4 is contrary to all Black's aims.

16.   cxb5

In general terms White does not want to lift the blockade of the c5 Pawn , but here he has a particularly incisive follow-up.

16.   ...   axb5
17.   a4!

The point. White recaptures control of the vital c4 square by force, for if now 17...c4 then simply 18. Rdd1 and the Pawn on c4 cannot be held.

17.   ...   bxa4

This lets the White Rooks loose, but 17...b4 18. Nc4 Ne8 is also dreadful for Black. It is no accident that White's

14

conquest of the c4 square is rapidly followed by the collapse of Black's game.

18.	Nc4	Ne8
19.	Rxa4	

Black's tortuous maneuvers (the Rook has moved to enable the Knight to defend the Bishop which defends his Pawns!) have maintained material equality, but left his King out in the cold. A typical example of the necessity to defend weaknesses drawing the defending forces out of position.

19.	...	Kb7

What else?

20.	f4!

The attack begins in earnest. If now 20...exf4, then 21. e5 Rf5! 22. Bxf4! Be7 (22...Rxf4 23. Nxd6+) 23. Na5+ gets to grips with the Black King.

20.	...	h6
21.	fxe5	hxg5
22.	exd6	cxd6

Or 22...Nxd6 23. Rb3+ Kc8 (23...Kb3 24. Ne5 mate) 24. Ne5 winning.

23.	Rb3+	Kc8
24.	Ra7	

Black is helpless against the threat of Rbb7 followed by Nb6+ mating. His pieces are mere spectators.

24.	...	d5
25.	exd5	Resigns.

The moral behind this trilogy of games should be clear: Look after your Pawns and your pieces will look after themselves. To 'look after' one's Pawns is not the most difficult thing in the world, and the next few chapters illustrate how this can be done and how the pieces can be made to cooperate with their Pawns.

2. Outposts

We all like to attack. There is a streak of sadism running through every chessplayer that helps him to sit back contentedly sipping a cup of tea while his opponent, head in hands, tries frantically to avert mate in three. But where do attacks come from? The mere action of pushing one or two pieces in the general direction of the enemy King does not constitute an attack. In general a successful attack can only be launched from a position of strength in the center of the board. This 'position of strength' can take various forms, the simplest being an outpost.

As the name suggests, an outpost is a square at the forefront of your position which you can readily support and from where you can control or contest squares in the heart of the enemy camp. To be useful an outpost must be firmly under control and so should ideally be protected by a Pawn. Conversely your opponent should not be given the opportunity to deny you access to your outpost, so in particular it must be *immune to attack by enemy pawns.*

This last condition is far and away the most important and can indeed almost be taken as the defining property of an outpost.

So as not to blur the issue with too many words let us look at some examples of outposts purely in terms of Pawn structure. In Diagram 7, there are plenty to be seen. White, from a structural point of view, has outposts on d5, b6, b4, g4. One might also regard c4 and a4 as outposts, for although they are not supported by Pawns, they certainly are immune from attack by them. Black has supported outposts on f4, g3, and unsupported ones on g5 and h5. You may have noticed that all of White's outposts are on the Queenside, Black's on the Kingside, so with such a Pawn structure one would normally expect to see White attacking on the left flank, and Black on the right.

This is all very theoretical and hypothetical, far from the stark realism of practice. For example, one rarely encounters the plethora of outposts seen in Diagram 7. You often have to be satisfied with one, or less!

7.

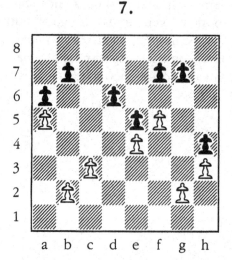

**1. e4 e5 2. Nf3 Nc6 3. Bb5 a6 4. Ba4 Nf6 5. 0-0 Be7
6. Re1 b5 7. Bb3 d6 8. c3 0-0 9. h3 Na5 10. Bc2 c5
11. d4 Nc6 12. Nbd2 Qb6 13. dxc5 dxc5**

8.

A quick look at the Pawn structure reveals that White
has one outpost (on d5), Black has none. However, life is not
quite so simple, as White is not the master of his c4 square, so
Black can at any time create an outpost on d3 by playing c4.
A typical state of affairs in these Ruy Lopez positions.

14.   Nf1

This Knight is the obvious candidate for residence on
d5, and so heads for the jumping-off square e3, from where it
incidentally also eyes the f5 square.

14.	...	Be6
15.	Ne3	Rad8
16.	Qe2	g6

9.

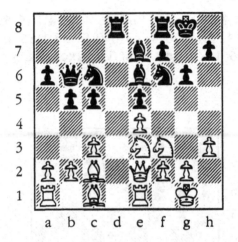

For the moment Bronstein has everything under control. White's outpost on d5 is well covered and his Knight has also been denied the f5 square. So what is there for White to do? The answer must be to harass the defenders of the d5 square.

17.   Ng5   c4!

Black quite rightly refuses to be bullied into retreating his Bishop. He fully realizes the importance of White's outpost on d5, and so is willing to allow his Pawns to be shattered by 18. Nxe6 fxe6 in order to take it away from him forever.

18.   a4

Unable to make any further headway in the center, Tal creates a diversion on the wing. In doing so he slightly weakens his own Queenside (Black now has an outpost on b3), but this is acceptable as the latent power of his d5 outpost prevents Black from undertaking anything active on the Queenside. If, for example, Black tries the natural 18...Nd7, heading for c5 and his own outposts on d3 and b3,

White's game suddenly springs to life with 18. axb5 axb5 19. Nd5!

18. ... Kg7

A useful move, improving his King position and waiting for White to show his hand.

19. axb5 axb5
20. Rb1

Preparing to challenge Black's Queenside supremacy with b3. The dissolution of Black's c Pawn would destroy his outposts before his pieces ever got near them.

White's maneuvers on the Queenside are not so much aimed at improving his own position as at eroding his opponent's—a sort of sabotage campaign.

20. ... Na5

To discourage b3.

21. Nf3!

A good time to admit that his Knight is serving no useful purpose on g5. As already pointed out, there is no future in taking the Bishop as Black recaptures with the Pawn and White's proud outpost is no more.

21. ... Qc7
22. Nd5!

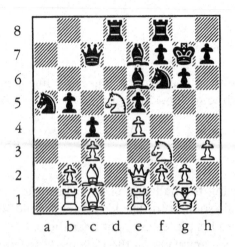

The moment we've all been waiting for, not to mention the White Queen, Rook and Bishop who have been patiently queuing up behind the e Pawn for some time. White's decision to play his trump card is now prompted by the fact that Black's Knight has been drawn out of play to a5. This may not seem to be very significant, but with the rapid opening up of the position which must surely follow, the absence of even a single piece from the central field of battle will cause great difficulties for Black.

22.   ...   Bxd5

The alternative 22...Nxd5 23. exd5 Bxd5 24. Nxe5 gives White a dangerous attack as he not only threatens to win a Pawn with 25. Nxg6, but also to launch a direct assault on the Black King with 25. Ng4 or 25. Qe3. A good example of an attack arising naturally from a "position of strength in the center", the position of strength in this case being the d5 square.

23.   exd5   Rfe8

A flexible move. He wants to see which way White

will take the e Pawn before deciding how to capture the d Pawn.

24.   Qxe5 Qxe5
25.   Nxe5 Nxd5
26.   Ra1

White's position is beginning to flow very smoothly.

26.   ...   Nb3
27.   Bxb3 cxb3
28.   Bh6+!

11.

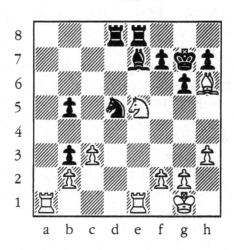

A stunning blow. If 28...Kxh6, then 29. Nxf7+ Kg7 30. Nxd8 Rxd8 31. Ra5 and Black is under great pressure. In the endgame an active Rook and a Pawn often outweigh Bishop and Knight, particularly so in this case as Black's Queenside Pawns are very vulnerable, e.g. 31...Rb8 32. Re5 Bd8 33. Ra3! (33. Ra7+ Nc7 may hold) picking off a second Pawn.

Notice the tremendous energy which has been released from the White position from 22. Nd5!.

28.	...	Kg8

Plagued by time trouble, Bronstein tries to play safe and runs into worse trouble. Grim though it may be, he must take the Bishop.

29.	Nc6	Rc8
30.	Rad1	Rxc6
31.	Rxd5	

There is no defense to the double threat of Rxe7 and Rxb5. The game concluded **31...f6 32. Rxb5 g5 33. Rxb3 Kf7 34. Rb7 Re6 35. Rxe6 Kxe6 36. h4 Rg8 37. f4 Bc5+ 38. Kf1 gxh4 39. Rb5 Rc8 40. f5+ Kd6 41. b4 h3 42. Rxc5 h2 43. Bf4+** resigns.

An instructive and exciting display of outpost play.

Particularly noteworthy was the terrible restraining influence exerted on Black by the continual 'threat' of Nd5. Having completed his development very harmoniously, Black found it extremely difficult to undertake any active plan without allowing the inevitable Nd5. Indeed, he only has to decentralize one piece (20...Na5) and the White Knight jumped down his throat.

We have just seen how an attack can spring from a central outpost. More obviously, an outpost in the vicinity of the enemy King is an excellent platform from which an offensive can be launched.

Benko-Najdorf, Los Angeles 1963

1. d4 Nf6 2. c4 c5 3. d5 d6 4. Nc3 g6 5. e4 Bg7 6. Be2 0-0 7. Nf3 e5 8. Bg5 h6 9. Bh4 g5 10. Bg3 Nh5 11. h4 Nf4 12. hxg5 hxg5 13. Bf1 Bg4 14. Qc2

12.

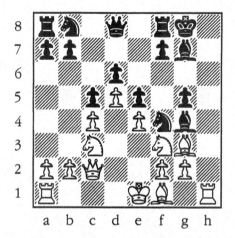

Black has mishandled the opening. True, he has firmly established his Knight on f4, but in doing so he has also given White an outpost on f5. An eye for an eye you might well say, but White's eye is dangerously near the Black King while the White King still has the right of abdication to the Queenside.

14.   ...   Bxf3?

A further misconception. Black needs this Bishop to have any chance of contesting the f5 square.

15.   gxf3   Nd7
16.   0-0-0

With the disappearance of the White King, Black's impressive-looking outpost on f4 bears little relevance to the position compared to White's. The one thing White must avoid is taking the Knight, as Black would gleefully recapture with the e Pawn thereby releasing his Bishop and giving himself outposts on e5 and d4.

16.   ...   Re8

Preparing to defend his Kingside with Nf8.

17. Bh3!

13.

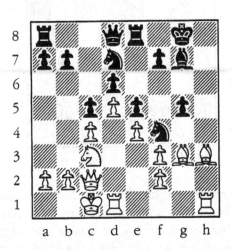

Bound for f5. If the Bishop is not taken, White can simply close his eyes and play Bf5, Rh2, Rdh1, Nd1-e3. When he opens them again, he is sure to find a win fairly quickly.

17.	...	Nxh3
18.	Rxh3	Nf8
19.	Rdh1	Ng6
20.	Nd1	Rc8
21.	Ne3	Rc7
22.	Nf5	Rf8
23.	Qd1	f6

Black is condemned to total passivity, whereas White can maneuver almost *ad infinitum* for an opening. Such positions are invariably lost for the defender in the long run, but here White immediately produces a neat and incisive finale.

24.   f4

14.

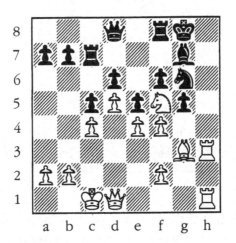

24.   ...   exf4
25.   Qh5!   Ne5

If 25...fxg3, then 26. Qxg6 and there is no way to avoid Rh8 mate, while 25...Kf7 26. Qh7 Rg8 27. Nh6+ also wins out of hand.

26.   Qh7+

Black resigns on account of 26...Kf7 27. Qxg7+ Ke8 28. Qxf8+ Kxf8 29. Rh8+ and 30. Rxd8

In most cases outposts, or potential outposts, are clearly apparent from the Pawn structure, but occasionally, a keen strategical eye is needed to realize the importance of a certain square. The Lord gave Botvinnik two very keen strategical eyes.

Botvinnik-Donner, Holland 1963

1. c4 Nf6 2. Nf3 e6 3. g3 d5 4. Bg2 Be7 5. 0-0 0-0 6. b3. b6 7. Bb2 Bb7 8. cxd5 Nxd5 9. d4 c5 10. dxc5 Bxc5 11. Nbd2 Nd7 12. a3 N(5)f6 13. b4 Be7

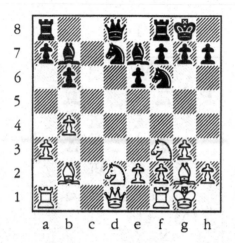

The center of the board appears to be a demilitarized zone and there is certainly no sign of any outposts. White's next move adds a new dimension to the position.

14.   Nd4!

Sensing that c6 can be made into an effective outpost for the Knight, as he can support it with a timely Pawn move to b5.

14.   ...   Bxg2

If he tries to cover the c6 square with 14...Nd5, then White replies 15. e4 N(5)f6 (15...Nc7 16. Rc1 secures the vital square) 16. e5 Nd5 17. Nc4 and White suddenly has an outpost on d6.

15.   Kxg2 Qc7
16.   Qb3   Rfc8

The right Rook to put on c8, as he may later want to challenge a White Pawn on b5 by a6.

17.   Rfc1   Qb7+
18.   Qf3!

An exchange of Queens would suit White very nicely—
18...Qxf3+ 19. N(2)xf3 followed by Nc6, Rc2, Rac1 with a
complete stranglehold on the game.

If White can ever establish his Knight on c6, the Black
Rooks will be suffocated.

18.   ...   Nd5!

A clever defensive maneuver designed to defend the
c6 square by blocking the long diagonal.

19.   e4   N(5)f6
20.   b5

16.

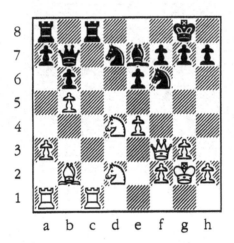

The struggle is reaching a critical point. Botvinnik has
completed his preparations for Nc6, so the question arises:
Can Black engineer enough exchanges to nullify the
smothering effect of Nc6? Let us look at some tries:

(i) 20...Rxc1 21. Rxc1 Rc8 22. Nc6! Bc5(or f8) is
precisely the kind of thing Black is trying to avoid. White

29

can follow up with 23. Nc4 and 24. Rd1, the advanced Knight rendering Black helpless against the build-up on the d file.

(ii) 20...Ne5(!) 21. Qe2 Rxc1 22. Rxc1 Rc8 23. Rxc8 Qxc8 24. f4 Ned7 25. Nc6 Bf8, when grabbing a Pawn with 26. Nxa7 would be reckless on account of the reply 27...Qc2!. Instead 26. Nc4 maintains White's initiative, but the total exchange of Rooks had eased the defense a little.

In the game, Donner tries a different approach which involves exchanging all the Rooks on the a file, but is surprised by White's 25th move.

20.	...	a6
21.	Nc6	Bf8
22.	a4	axb5
23.	axb5	Rxa1
24.	Rxa1	Ra8

17.

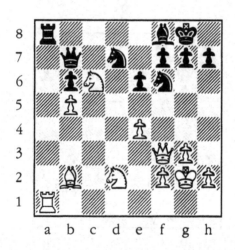

25. Rd1!

A deep move. Botvinnik realizes that his opponent can do little on the a file (25...Ra2 26. Qb3 or even 26. Nc4) and that he needs a pair of Rooks on the board to make full use of his outposts.

25.   ...   Ne8

A symptom of White's pressure. His Queenside advance has left Black with an outpost on c5, but the immediate occupation with 25...Nc5 loses a Pawn after 26. Bxf6.

26.   Nc4   Nc5
27.   e5

Unveiling some deadly tactical possibilities on the long diagonal, which lead Black in virtual *zugzwang*, viz.

(i) 27...Nc7 28. Rd7! Nxd7 29. Ne7+ winning the Queen.

(ii) 27...Na4 28. Ne7+! Qxe7 29. Qxa8

(iii) 27...Ra4 28. Rd8 Rxc4 29. Rxe8 with the deadly threat of Ne7+.

(iv) 27...Kh8 (to cut out the Ne7+ possibilities) 28. Nxb6! Qxb6 29. Qxf7 and the Bishop is lost (29...Nc7 30. Rd8!).

You may wonder why all these combinations are suddenly bouncing into the picture. The answer is that combination possibilities almost invariably accompany an overwhelming positional superiority, such as the one White has here.

27.   ...   Rc8
28.   Ra1

Wins! The threat is Ra7 winning the Queen, and 28...Ra8 loses to 29. Rxa8 Qxa8 30. Ne7+, a familiar theme.

28.   ...   Rc7

Or 28...Qc7 29. Ra7 Nb7 30. Bd4 Bc5 31. Bxc5 bxc5 32. N(c6)a5

29.   Ra7   Qxa7
30.   Nxa7   Rxa7
31.   Nxb6 Resigns.

Thus far we have seen how an outpost can act as a pivot about which the game swings to and fro. Rather like the trunk of a tree, an outpost is a central pillar from which branches of attack grow naturally. You only have to be careful that you do not choose a branch that breaks off as you crawl along it. Fine, but what happens when you sit at the board and you have no outpost? You can build one.

Fischer-Gadia, Mar del Plata 1960

1. e4 c5 2. Nf3 d6 3. d4 cxd4 4. Nxd4 Nf6 5. Nc3 a6 6. Bc4 e6 7. Bb3 b5 8. 0-0 Bb7 9. f4 Nc6? (9...Nbd7) 10. Nxc6 Bxc6

18.

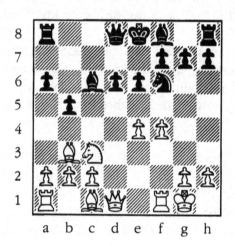

White has no outpost and his e Pawn is hanging, but he does have a lead in development. If he tries to utilize this by blindly hacking his way through the center with 11. e5? he will not be impressed with the result after 11...dxe5 12. fxe5 Bc5+ 13. Kh1 Qxd1 14. Rxd1 Ng4. A bit more subtlety is required—he needs an outpost, so...

11.   f5!   e5

Giving way without a fight. Less obliging is 10...Qd7, though after 11. fxe6 fxe6 12. Qd4! Be7 13. Bg5 White has an enduring initiative, if no outpost as yet.

Black's most interesting move here is 10...b4 trying to drive the Knight well away from d5 before conceding the square, i.e. 10...b4 11. Na4 e5! and White's outpost is a little used to him as he cannot occupy it. This idea would work very well for Black were it not that he is mauled by the piece sacrifice 10...b4 11. fxe6! bxc3 12. exf7+ Ke7 (12...Kd7 13. e5) 13. Qe1! Some sample lines:

(i) 13...cxb2 14. Bxb2 (threatening e5) Nxe4 15. Rf4 d5 16. Rxe4+! dxe4 17. Ba3+ with a savage attack.

(ii) 13...Qb6+ 14. Be3 Qb7 15. e5! dxe5 16. Qxc3 etc.

(iii) 13...Qc7 14. Qxc3 Nxe4 15. Qh3 and Black has terrible problems.

I give these lines to illustrate the role played by White's development advantage. It is not in itself sufficient to force home a mating attack, but it does force Black to make positional concessions (conceding the d4 square) in order to avoid meeting a grisly end. Attacking play and positional play are not incompatible opposites. On the contrary, they go hand in hand.

12.   Qd3

His positional goal (an outpost) attained, White must return to more mundane affairs namely the defense of his e Pawn.

12.   ...   Be7
13.   Bg5!

When an outpost has been setup the next and most logical thing to do is chase off, exchange, or harass defending pieces which cover the square in question. Here White takes the opportunity to trade his Black-square Bishop (which can never itself control d5) for the enemy Knight which does control d5, thereby making his outpost an absolutely permanent feature of the position. Black could and probably should have prevented this with 12...h6.

13.	...	Qb6+
14.	Kh1	0-0
15.	Bxf6	

All according to plan.

| 15. | ... | Bxf6 |
| 16. | Bd5! | |

Beautifully simple. The last defender of d5 is eliminated.

16.	...	Rac8
17.	Bxc6	Rxc6
18.	Rad1	

The final preparation for Nd5 which if played at once could be met by 18...Qd4! 19. Qxd4 exd4 and Black has good chances to save the endgame as the White e and c Pawns are rather weak.

18.	...	Rfc8
19.	Nd5	Qd8
20.	c3	

19.

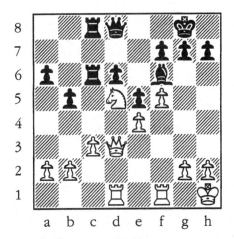

"This is the kind of position I get in my dreams," was Fischer's comment on reaching a position similar to this one as White in a skittles game against the late Russian Grandmaster, Leonid Stein. Fischer then proceeded to prove that even he is human by losing it. In fact, the position Fischer remarked upon was much less favorable for White than this one. Here, the White Knight seemingly dominates the whole board and is completely unassailable. Black cannot exchange it off for anything less than a Rook, but can undertake nothing while the tyrannical beast rules.

20.	...	Be7
21.	Ra1!	

What bridge players term as a safety play. White can virtually win this position as he pleases, but Fischer characteristically chooses the line of minimum risk. His plan is simply to play a4 and Black's Queenside Pawns will prove to be indefensible.

A more adventurous, but less scientific, approach would be 21. f6 Bxf6 22. Rxf6!? gxf6 23. Rf1 with a strong attack.

21.	...	f6

This loses, but so does everything else, e.g. 21...Bf8 22. a4 bxa4 (22...Rb8 23. Nb4 Rcb6 24. a5 R(6)b7 25. Nc6) 23. Rxa4 and the a Pawn soon falls.

22.	a4	Rb8??

Black is losing a Pawn at least, but evidently not one to do things by halves, he gives away a Rook instead.

23.	Nxe7+ Resigns

On account of 23...Qxe7 24. Qd5+.

We have so far seen illustrations of how to set up, secure and exploit outposts, but no clue has been given as how to play *against* an outpost. The most usual way to counter an enemy outpost is to cover it with as many pieces as possible so that when he occupies it with a piece, you can capture enough times to force him eventually to recapture with a Pawn.

20.

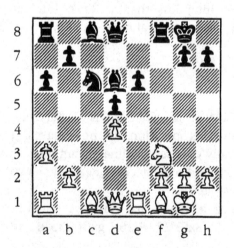

For example, in Diagram 20, White has an outpost on

e5, but Ne5 can always be met by Nxe5 and after recapturing with the Pawn, his outpost is gone. Clearly he needs to bring another minor piece to bear on e5, so White to move would play 1. Bg5 and follow it up with Bh4 and Bg3. If on the other hand Black is on the move, he would seek to prevent this. 1...h6 is the obvious way, but a more active solution is preferable—namely 1...Qe8 (so as to meet 2. Bg5 with 2...Qh5! threatening Rxf3) or 1...Qb6. Either move gives Black a fine position.

21.

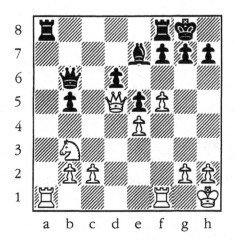

If you are unable to cover your opponent's outpost, then extremely active harassing tactics are needed. Diagram 21 shows a marked structural resemblance to Diagram 19, but the position features a vital difference—the White Knight has not yet reached d5. Indeed it is at least four moves away. This gives Black some breathing space, which he must make good use of. After the Knight reaches d5 he is lost.

The diagrammed position occurred in the game Unzicker-Fischer, Varna 1962. Fischer continued:

1.   ...   Ra4!

Immobilizing the Knight (2. Nd2? Rd4).

2.   c3   Qa6

Not falling to the trap 2...Rfa8 3. Qxa8+!

3.   h3?

Relieving the non-existent back rank threats. He should play 3. Rad1, threatening Nc1, Nd3, and Nb4.

3.   ...   Rc8
4.   Rfe1   h6
5.   Kh2

White is playing planlessly. He may have been intending 5. Rxa4 bxa4 6. Nc1, but 6...a3 sees Black breaking through on the Queenside.

5.   ...   Bg5

Black's position is looking very good.

6.   g3?   Qa7
7.   Kg2   Ra2!

With the double threat of Rxb2+ and Rxc3. Surprisingly there's no defense.

8.   Kf1   Rxc3!

Resigns, as after 9. Rxa2 (9. bxc3 Qf2 mate) Rf3+ 10. Ke2 Rf2+ 11. Kd1 Qxa2 his position is wrecked. The poor Knight never even moved!

The lesson to be learned here is that structure alone is not quite everything. The pieces must be able to coordinate with the Pawn structure. After all, what use is a body without a soul?

3. Weak Pawns

In the previous chapter we looked at Pawn structure from the point of view of outposts and how an outpost acts as a pivot, about which the pieces can swing into action. Without such an outpost as foundation, pieces tend to lack the stability necessary for a successful assault and are liable to be driven back in confusion. It is sheer folly to try to attack directly a well coordinated and developed position. Many players underestimate the defensive resources inherent in such positions and will in game after game bash their heads against a brick wall instead of using their heads to first weaken the cement. The point they repeatedly fail to appreciate is that a very definite superiority in force is needed to ensure that an attack will be successful. This superiority can take either one of two forms:

(i) Better development. This is simply a case of superiority in numbers, the aggressor being able to feed more pieces into the attack than the defender has available to fight them off.

(ii) Better coordination. This is a much more subtle form of advantage which one must work hard to build up. The idea is to disarm the defense by first tying its pieces down to the defense of certain points, so that when the storm does break they have very little scope or opportunity to react.

Here we concern ourselves primarily with the second condition. Outposts provide the necessary stability for the attacker, but something must also be done to destroy the defender's coordination. This is where the second aspect of Pawn structure, weak Pawns, comes in. If the defending forces can be reduced to the menial task of protecting Pawns, they will not be able to offer much opposition to a full-scale offensive.

So what exactly is a weak Pawn and how is it recognizable? The answer is both simple and logical. A weak Pawn is one which cannot be protected by another Pawn and so requires support from its own pieces. Note .

39

that the criterion is the *ability* to be protected by another Pawn, not the existence of such protection. Take the example of two adjacent Pawns on, say, d4 and e4. Neither protects the other but each has the ability to be guarded by the other, by advancing. We must therefore say that the weakness or strength of two adjacent Pawns depends on whether or not they are able to advance if the necessity arises.

22.

Diagram 22 gives us an example of adjacent Pawns (d6, c6) which are very definitely weak, because neither can move. d5 is never feasible, as it leaves the e Pawn in the soup after the reply exd5 (note for this purpose the power of the White Rook on e1), while c5 leaves Black riddled with holes. The continuation of the game Hecht-Forintos illustrates well the combination of outpost play (f5) and the exploitation of weak Pawns.

1.   Bg5

A simple developing move which exerts great pressure on the Black Pawns. White has many threats to win a Pawn, including the spectacular 2. Nxe5!

40

| 1. | ... | Rfd8 |

Black has no choice but to defend passively. If he tries to iron out his weaknesses with 1...Bxg5 2. Nxg5 d5, he merely tees himself up for the knockout punch, viz. 3. Qh5 h6, and now White can win spectacularly by 4. Nxh6+ gxh6 5. Qxh6 Rfe8 (forced) 6. Re3! with a winning attack for the piece, or settle for the methodical 4. Nxf7 Qxf7 5. Qxg6! Qxg6 6. Ne7+ Kh7 7. Nxg6 Kxg6 8. exd5 winning a Pawn.

Athought White cannot hope to achieve success by a direct Kingside attack, Black's frantic attempts to cover up his weaknesses could well set something up for him.

| 2. | Rc1 | |

Turning the focus of attention to the c Pawn (he threatens to win it by capturing twice on e7), while preserving the harmony of the White position.

| 2. | ... | Rac8 |
| 3. | Rc3! | |

A multipurpose move illustrating clearly the maleffects of weak Pawns. White creates options to double on the c file (with Qc2), double on the d file (Rd3) or possibly transfer the Rook to g3 at some later date. Black has no opportunity to reciprocate, but must on every move be prepared to meet each contingency. We see a definite rift between the mobility of the two armies opening up. When the gap becomes wide enough White will be able to bludgeon his way through the Black position without encountering much resistance.

3.	...	Bxg5
4.	Nxg5	Nf4
5.	g3	Bh5

If 5...Ne6, 6. Qg4 is extremely unpleasant for Black.

41

6.	Qd2	Ne6
7.	Nxe6	Qxe6
8.	Qg5	

Suddenly it's all over. There are three different threats (Qxg7 mate, Qxh5 Ne7+) and no defense to all of them.

The speed of capitulation should make it abundantly clear that pieces tied to the defense of weak Pawns are often unable to defend themselves.

The most common form of Pawn weakness encountered in practical play is the isolated Pawn—one which has lost its neighbors and stands alone in face of the enemy. Such a Pawn has two basic deficiencies: firstly it requires defense, and secondly the squares immediately in front of it make ideal outposts for the other player. To see in more tangible terms what this means, let us look at a famous game Fischer won on his road to the World Championship against an ex-World Champion Tigran Petrosian.

White: Fisher, Black: Petrosian
Candidate's Match (Game 7), Buenos Aires 1971

1.	e4	c5
2.	Nf3	e6
3.	d4	cxd4
4.	Nxd4	a6
5.	Bd3	Nc6
6.	Nxc6	bxc6
7.	0-0	d5
8.	c4	

23.

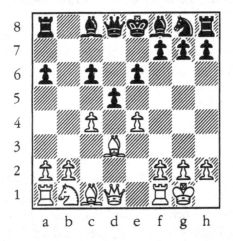

Black has built up a very solid-looking Pawn center, but only at the cost of neglecting his development. Fischer uses the time he has gained, not to launch any violent offensive (Black's position is quite solid enough to absorb anything like that), but to break up the Black center before its pieces have the chance to support it. A Pawn center must be adequately supported by pieces to be effective, else it merely becomes a target to attack.

8.   ...   Nf6

Under no circumstances can Black consider recapturing away from d5, as this would leave him with 'split' Pawns on a6, c6 whose weakness would plague him for the rest of the game. A plausible alternative was 8...d4, trying to keep the center closed, but yet another non-developing move must be regarded with some suspicion.

9.   cxd5 cxd5
10.   exd5 exd5

Ideally Black would prefer to recapture with the

Knight, but after the reply 11. Be4! he would in the long run be unable to avoid the isolation of his Pawn owing to the pin on the diagonal.

Having successfully saddled Black with two isolated Pawns, Fischer now gives us a perfect lesson in how to go about taking full advantage of them.

11. Nc3 Be7
12. Qa4+!

A deep move. Given time to castle, play Bb7 and d4, Black would be very happy. Remember, weak Pawns are only a handicap if they result in the pieces being driven to bad or passive squares in order to defend them. Now however, 12...Bd7 13. Qd4 gives the White Queen a dominating view of the world while leaving the Black pieces hemmed in behind the d Pawn. Rather than submit to this, Petrosian sets a cunning trap.

12. ... Qd7!?
13. Re1!

Fischer does not allow his vision to be blurred by a lust for materialism. He could win the exchange by 13. Bb5 axb5 14. Qxa8, but after 14...0-0, ...Bb7 and ...d4 Black's whole position suddenly springs to life and White finds himself in trouble. Always be wary of grabbing material at the cost of the coordination of your pieces.

13. ... Qxa4
14. Nxa4 Be6
15. Be3 0-0

24.

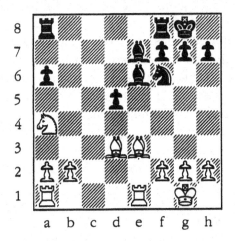

A convenient time to stop and reassess the situation. The exchange of Queens has helped White somewhat, in that without Queens less can happen to interrupt or obscure the basic flow of the game. Nevertheless White's overall strategy remains unchanged. He must use the weakness of the two isolated Pawns to tie down the Black pieces while maximizing the activity of his own.

16.   Bc5

One of the secrets of endgame play is to realize which pieces to exchange, which to retain. Here White wants to trade off the Black-squared Bishops for two reasons:

(i) As the weak Pawns stand on White squares, the Black-squared Bishop is the only piece which *cannot* be tied down to their defense.

(ii) White wants to use the c5 square as an outpost for his Knight.

16.	...	Rfe8
17.	Bxe7	Rxe7
18.	b4!	

45

The next logical step in the chain. Having just traded the 'right' pair of Bishops, he does not want the Black Pawns to run away onto Black squares, for in that case he will have traded the wrong Bishops! Now White can always meet ...a5 with b5 and the massive passed Pawn must prove decisive. This process of fixing weaknesses on squares where they are most readily assailable is particularly common and should always be borne in mind when playing against weak Pawns.

It is also worth noting that b4 establishes the outpost on c5. Whether you approach the position from the point of view of outposts or weaknesses, the move 18. b4! cries out to be played.

18. ...   Kf8

In endgames the King is a very powerful piece and should be used as such. The immediate value of this move is to unpin the Bishop, but in the longer term Black would like to bring his King to d6 from where it would probably cement his position together.

19. Nc5   Bc8
20. f3

White also needs to use his King. Despite the fact that each of his pieces is more actively placed than its opposite number there is no immediate way to break through, so the King must be used to increase the pressure.

Mistaken would be 20. Rxe7 Kxe7 21. Re1+ Kd6 when Black can probably hold the position. It is important not to allow the Black King across the e file. Once on the Queenside it can to some extent release the pieces from their task of defending Pawns for more active service.

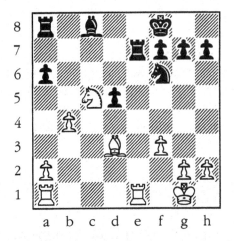

25

20.   ...   Rea7

A very curious move, but its motivation is worth closer study. There are no points in the White position to counter attack, so Black must seek some method of 'improving' his own position. The obvious try is to bring the King to d6, but the only available route Ke8, Kd8, Kc7, Kd6 is both long and hazardous. The other possibility is to transfer the Bishop to a more active defensive post. At the moment the Bishop effectively defends the a Pawn, but plays no further part in the game, other than interfering with the Rooks' coordination and generally getting in the way.

It could fulfill its duties much more efficiently from b5, but the problem is how to get there. The normal try would be 20...Nd7 21. Nb3 (exchanges help the defense) 22. Bf1 Bd7 intending Bb5 on the next turn. At this point however the weakness of the d Pawn takes its toll, for after 23. Red1 (not 23. Rad1 Bb5 24. Rxd5? Nxf3+!) Black must abandon his plan in order to save the Pawn. Petrosian's move has the same idea (Bd7, Bb5) in mind.

21.   Re5   Bd7

According to plan.

22. Nxd7+

A slightly surprising decision in that one would not normally want to trade such a dominating Knight for a struggling Bishop, but here the exchange enables Fischer to penetrate with his Rooks. It is really a question of trading one advantage (superior minor piece) for another (superior Rooks).

22. ... Rxd7
23. Rc1 Rd6

To try to free the other Rook from the defense of the a Pawn.

24. Rc7 Nd7
25. Re2 g6

Black has been totally starved of constructive moves. Let us examine the position in detail to see why:
    (a) If the Knight moves, there comes Ree7 winning.
    (b) King moves also allow Re7.
    (c) If Black tried to trade off his passive Rook with 25...Re8, White would complete the tying-up process by 26. Rxe8+ Kxe8 27. Ra7 Nb8 28. b5! (There are other ways to win, but this is the neatest) 28...axb5 29. Bxb5+ Kf8 (29...Nd7) leads to a lost King and Pawn endgame after 30. Kf2 Kd8 31. Bxd7 Rxd7 32. Rxd7+ Kxd7 33. Ke3 Kd6 34. Kd4 etc.) 30. Rb7! Rd8 31. Kf2 and Black has no moves at all. White simply blockades the d Pawn with his King and Queens the a Pawn.
    (d) Obviously the Rook on d6 cannot move.
    (e) 25...a5 26. Bb5 N moves 27. Ree7 etc.
The necessity to guard two isolated Pawns has reduced Black to Pawn moves alone. White now only has to add one more weight, namely his King, and the scales must tip.

| 26. | Kf2 | h5 |
| 27. | f4 | |

With the idea Kg3, Kh4, Kg5 and f5.

27.	...	h4
28.	Kf3	f5
29.	Ke3	

The King has been denied an entrance on the Kingside, but the chessboard is a big place. There is plenty of room on the other side.

| 29. | ... | d4+ |

Naturally Kd4 must be prevented.

| 30. | Kd2 | Nb6 |

Rather than wait for the King to ooze in, Petrosian makes a final bid for some counterplay. Purely passive defense would lose to, *inter alia*, the plan of Bc4, Kd3 and Re6.

31.	Ree7	Nd5
32.	Rf7+	Ke8
33.	Rb7	Nxf4
34.	Bc4!	Black resigns.

26.

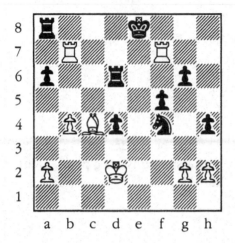

A quaint final position which shows the immense power of even a small coordinated force. Despite having a Pawn more, Black is quite helpless in face of the threat of Rg7 and Rg8 mate. E.g. 34...g5 35. Rg7 Rf6 (35...Ng6 36. Bf7+) 36. Rg8+ Rf8 37 Bf7+.

A truly classic game, one worth continual restudy. It shows with perfect simplicity all the steps necessary to transform a superior Pawn structure into a win. The one underlying theme running through the whole game is the way the Black pieces are systematically deprived of all mobility.

27.

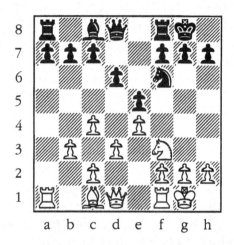

Next we look at doubled Pawns, a subject littered with common misconceptions. Contrary to popular belief, doubled Pawns are not invariably weak but in many cases are definitely advantageous. Naturally doubled *isolated* Pawns are to be avoided, but there is no reason to fear having doubled Pawns when no isolation of Pawns occurs.

For example, in the following line of the Vienna Opening 1. e4 e5 2. Nc3 Nf6 3. Bc4 Nc6 4. d3 Bb4 5. Nf3 d6 6. 0-0 Bxc3 7. bxc3 Na5 8. Bb3 Nxb3 9. axb3 0-0 10. c4 (Diagram 27), the only effect of the doubled Pawns is to give White a small but unquestionable advantage. Why? Basically because White has more central Pawns than his opponent (he leads by two c Pawns to one). In the opening and middlegame center Pawns are more valuable than flank Pawns. Moreover the White Pawns provide a very effective barrier against the enemy Bishop without any way impeding their own Bishop. Above all there is no question of White having any weak Pawns—they all protect each other, except for the 'base' at c2 which is completely unassailable. There is of course very little wrong with the Black position either, but the Danish Grandmaster Bent Larsen has been able to turn White's slender advantage into a win. It requires infinite patience and perfect technique, but it is possible.

The pros and cons of doubled Pawns may be thought of in terms of a military line along which forces are evenly distributed. One can reinforce a certain part of the line only at the cost of weakening another. Naturally the value of the policy depends on how serious the weakening effect is. To translate this notion into chess terms consider the Pawn complex e3, f3, f2, h2. The Pawn triplet on e3, f3, f2, is by itself quite strong as it controls a lot of central squares without exhibiting much to attack. The weakness lies with the isolated h Pawn and the squares in front of it. Returning to the context of our analogy we can say that the center has been strengthened at the cost of weakening the flank. If the latter effect turns out to be inconsequential then the doubling of the Pawns must be reckoned to be a good thing.

Aron Nimzowitsch was maybe one of the first to have a deep understanding of doubled Pawns. A great chess thinker and experimentalist, he pioneered what is nowadays generally considered to be the 'perfect' defense to 1. d4, namely 1...Nf6 2. c4 e6 3. Nc3 Bb4—the Nimzo-Indian. Black's basic strategy is to take the Knight at the right moment, doubling White's c Pawns and then try to prove that they are weak. Naturally this idea has received many ramifications over the years, but it can still be made to work even at the highest levels.

White: B. Spassky, Black: R. J. Fischer
5th Match Game, Reykjavik 1972

1.	d4	Nf6
2.	c4	e6
3.	Nc3	Bb4
4.	Nf3	c5
5.	e3	Nc6
6.	Bd3	Bxc3+
7.	Bxc3	d6

Having traded off his Bishop to double the Pawns,

Black must be careful to contain the enemy Bishop on c1. This he does by setting up his central Pawns on *Black squares* to reduce the Bishop's scope.

8.	e4	e5
9.	d5	Ne7
10.	Nh4	

Preparing to open lines for his Bishops with f4. He can meet 10...Ng6 with 11. Nf5

10.	...	h6
11.	f4	Ng6!

Black is himself willing to accept doubled Pawns to open lines for his pieces. In a few moves we shall see exactly why.

12.	Nxg6	fxg6
13.	fxe5?!	

This helps Black. Better is to keep the tension with 13. 0-0.

13.	...	dxe5
14.	Be3	b6
15.	0-0	0-0
16.	a4	a5!

28.

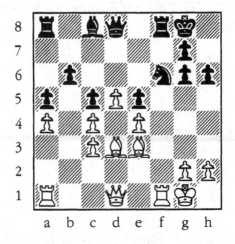

Black has given himself a backward b Pawn, an isolated e Pawn and doubled g Pawns. Why? To keep the position blocked. The White Bishops are badly hemmed in by their own Pawns and without prospect of ever breaking out. We have here a new source of 'weakness'. White's Pawns are bad not so much because they require defense, but simply because they get in the way. In some sense one can think of them being weak because the pieces cannot avoid defending them.

17.	Rb1	Bd7
18.	Rb2	Rb8
19.	Rbf2	Qe7
20.	Bc2	

White has already run out of constructive ideas. Although his pieces are all very well placed, they have no effect because they cannot cooperate with the Pawns. The game has already been reduced to a question of whether Black can create enough threats to win. White can only wait.

20.	...	g5

21.	Bd2	Qe8
22.	Be1	Qg6
23.	Qd3	Nh5

The first attempt to make progress. Black's Knight heads for a semi-outpost on f4. I use the term semi-outpost because White can defend that point with a Pawn (g3), but does not want to unless absolutely necessary because it leaves a hole for Black's Bishop on h3 in dangerous proximity to the King.

24.	Rxf8+	Rxf8
25.	Rxf8+	Kxf8
26.	Bd1	Nf4
27.	Qc2??	

29.

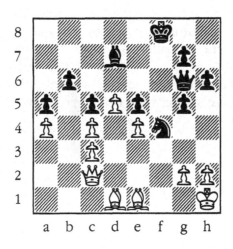

An outright blunder losing immediately. He must play 27. Qb1 when the White position is bad, but difficult to crack. However, the psychological effects of having to hold a prospectless position for what might seem an infinite amount of time does nothing to aid the defender's concentration.

27.   ...   Bxa4!

White resigns. After 28. Qxa4 Qxe4 he loses everything. A game decided by Pawns, not pieces.

Of course one cannot play the Nimzo-Indian with the *idee fixe* of doubling White's c Pawns at all costs. An auxiliary strategy is needed, as White can always decide not to accept double Pawns if he so wishes.

White: S. J. Hutchings, Black: R. D. Keene
Woolacomb 1973

1.	c4	Nf6
2.	Nc3	b6
3.	Nf3	Bb7
4.	d4	e6
5.	g3	Bb4

White is a little confused by Black's unusual move order (2...b6) and has allowed transposition into a Nimzo-Indian in which he is committed to fianchettoing his f1 Bishop. The King side fianchetto is not altogether desirable against the Nimzo, as the White Pawn on c4 lacks support with the Bishop on g2.

6.   Bd2

Opting to avoid the double Pawns, but only at the cost of some time.

6.   ...   c5

Plan B. Black utilizes the time he has gained to switch to an attack on White's center, using the power of the fianchettoed Bishop.

7.   a3

Although this simultaneously acquires the two Bishops and succeeds in defending the center, it also represents a further loss of time. Less ambitious but safer was 7. dxc5 and 8. Bg2.

7.	...	Bxc3
8.	Bxc3	Ne4!

Back to Plan A. The prospect of doubled c Pawns is just as unpalatable as before, so White is tempted to waste still more time to avoid being saddled with them.

9.	Qc2	Nxc3
10.	Qxc3	Qf6

30.

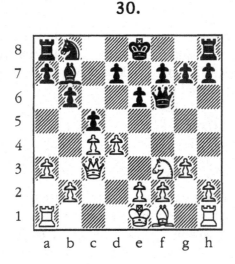

There is something vaguely symphonic about this course of this game. We are given the first subject (threat to double c Pawns), second subject (attack on d4), then the first again and now we have both of them together! The threat is ...Bxf3 winning a Pawn and White dare not capture away from d4 because of the double Pawns he would have to endure after ...Qxc3+.

11.   Rd1   Bxf3!

A fine move that tells us much about doubled Pawns. Black is not doubling White's f Pawns in order to attack them, but to create an outpost for his Knight on d4. The quartet of Pawns on f2, f3, g3, h2 in itself forms a very strong Pawn complex, but the metamorphosis of White's e Pawn into an f Pawn means that he can no longer control his d4 square. We can see exactly the same idea in a game Karpov-Browne, San Antonio 1972, which opened 1. c4 c5 2. b3!? Nf6 3. Bb2 g6?! 4. Bxf6! exf6 5. Nc3 and White has a beautiful outpost on d5. Recall the analogy with the military line. The effect here of doubling the Pawns is to strengthen the flank, but weakens the center.

12.   Qxf3

Still determined to avoid the dreaded doubled c Pawns. Understandably so, as after the alternative 12. exf3 Nc6 13. d5 Qxc3+ 14. bxc3 Na5 his Pawn structure does have a very unkept appearance.

12.   ...   Qxf3
13.   exf3   Nc6
14.   dxc5?

But this is a serious mistake. Admittedly 14. d5 Nd4 is good for Black because of his powerful Knight, but it at least does not offer him any obvious point of attack. The text move however opens the b file and so leaves White with a *backward* b Pawn open to attack along the file. The fact that it opens the d file for White is irrelevant here as the Black King comfortably thwarts any aspirations he might have in that direction.

14.   ...   bxc5
15.   Bg2   Rb8
16.   Rd2   Rb3!

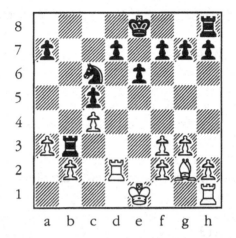

31

Displaying the second feature of a backward Pawn on an open file, namely that the square in front of it makes a splendid outpost. With an advanced outpost for his Rook, one for his Knight, and a backward Pawn to attack Black has, positionally speaking, everything he could ever ask for.

17.   Kd1

White's only hope is to try and hold the b file with his King. Incidentally, his last move sets a little trap. Black can apparently now pick up a Pawn with 17...Ne5. Indeed so, but after 18. Kc2 Nxf3 (or ...18. Nxc4) 19. Kxb3 Nxd2+ 20. Kc3! White picks up a Knight.

17.   ...   Ke7
18.   f4   Nd4
19.   Kc1   h5!?

Black is also capable of setting traps, but this one is much more subtle. The automatic choice of move here is 19...Rhb8, but first he creates a diversion. We shall presently see why.

20.   h4

Why not prevent ...h4? It can't do any harm, can it?

20.   ...   Rhb8
21.   Bf1

The penny drops. Black is threatening to pull off the *coup* 21...Rxg3!! 22. fxg3 Nb3+ 23. Kd1 Nxd2 24. Kxd2 Rxb2+ and 25...Rxg2. To set this combination up he had to lure the h Pawn away from h2, so that ...Rxg3 could not be recaptured with the h Pawn, in which case he would unable to pick up the Bishop at the end.

21.   ...   Rf3

Decisive infiltration. The threat is simply 22...Nb3+.

22.   Kd1   Rxa3!

Another elegant blow (23. bxa3 Rb1 mate) and indeed the last one, as White resigns at this juncture to avoid any further humiliation.

In recent times there has been a trend to go to almost any lengths in order to weaken enemy Pawns, especially to inflict doubled isolated Pawns. The first victim of this trend was the previously much revered fianchettoed g2 or g7 Bishop. For example: 1. c4 g6 2. Nc3 Bg7 3. Nf3 c5 4. d4 cxd4 5. Nxd4 Nc6 6. Nc2 Bxc3+! (the classical chess theorist might advocate exchanging this piece for nothing less than a Rook!) 7. bxc3 Nf6 followed by going to work on the Pawns with ...d6, ...Be6, ...Rc8, ...Ne5 (or a5) etc. A double-edged idea as Black's Kingside is severely weakened by the loss of its Bishop, but one that seems to work well enough in practice.

Similarly Petrosian's idea in the English opening:
1. c4 Nf6 2. Nc3 g6 3. g3 d5 4. cxd5 Nxd5 5. Bg2 Nb6 6. d3! (delaying the development of his g1 Knight so that he can

give up his Bishop for the Black Knight when it comes out of hiding) 6...Bg7 7. Be3 Nc6 8. Bxc6+! bxc6 9. Qc1.

Even the Rook is sometimes called upon to lay down its life to split up some Pawns. For example, in the following well-known line of the Dragon-Sicilian: 1. e4 c5 2. Nf3 d6 3. d4 cxd4 4. Nxd4 Nf6 5. Nc3 g6 6. Be3 Bg7 7. f3 Nc6 8. Qd2 0-0 9. Bc4 Bd7 10. h4 h5 11. 0-0-0 Rc8 12. Bb3 Ne5 13. Bh6, Black nonchalantly continues with 13...Bxh6 14. Qxh6 Rxc3! 15. bxc3 Qc7 with a perfectly good game despite having a whole exchange less.

To conclude this section we look at a complex struggle between a World Champion and ex-World Champion which highlights the tendency of weak Pawns always to have the last word, even when there seems to be some counterplay about.

White: A. Karpov, Black: B. Spassky
Spartakiad 1975

1.	d4	Nf6
2.	c4	e6
3.	Nf3	b6
4.	g3	Bb7
5.	Bg2	Be7
6.	Nc3	0-0
7.	Qc2	d5

Black must challenge the center before e4 comes. The alternative 7...c5 is less good as White can counter with the following ingenious maneuver: 8. d5 exd5 9. Ng5! (White wants to recapture on d5 with a piece so as to make an outpost there) 9...Nc6 10. Nxd5 g6 11. Qd2 and White stands better because of his outpost on d5. Playing the Black side of this in his match against Korchnoi, Karpov continued 11...Nxd5 12. Bxd5 Rb8? overlooking the winning combination 13. Nxh7 (the Knight cannot be taken because of 14. Qh6+ Kg8 15. Qxg6+ Kh8 16. Qh6+ Kg8 17. Be4 f5 18. Bd5+ Rf7 19. Qg6+).

8.	cxd5	Nxd5
9.	0-0	Nd7
10.	Nxd5	

A well-timed exchange, as 10...Bxd5 11. e4 Bb7 12. Rd1 gives White an impressive center. Consequently Black decides after all to block his Bishop by recapturing with the Pawn.

10.	...	exd5
11.	Rd1	

32.

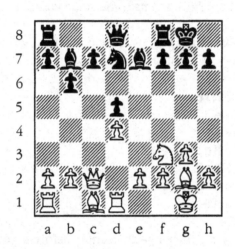

Anticipating the freeing move ...c5, Karpov envisages that the Black Pawn on d5 may well become weak. There is at the moment no compulsion for Black to break out with c5, but he will find it difficult to avoid forever.

11.	...	Nf6
12.	Ne5	

Now, however, White threatens to establish an outpost on c6, so Black has little choice in the matter.

| 12. | ... | c5 |
| 13. | dxc5 | Bxc5 |

Spasky avoids the so-called 'hanging Pawns' which would result from 13...bxc5. Generally speaking hanging Pawns are strong so long as they can be maintained together (i.e. on c5, d5), but if one is forced to advance, the rear one becomes very weak. Here White would be immediately able to break up the hanging Pawns (after 13...bxc5) by 14. e4 d4 15 Nc4 obtaining an outpost for the Knight. On the other hand, the isolated Pawn Black now acquires is an obvious target, moreover a stationary one on account of the pin on the long diagonal (g2 b7).

| 14. | Nd3 | Bd6 |
| 15. | Bf4 | |

We have seen before (cf. Fischer-Petrosian) this idea of exchanging Black's active Bishop, leaving only the passive defender on the board.

15.	...	Re8
16.	e3	Ne4
17.	Bxd6	Qxd6
18.	Nf4	

A very good square for the Knight. The pressure on Black's d Pawn is obvious, but he is not without some counterchances based on his own well-placed Knight.

| 18. | ... | Rac8 |
| 19. | Qa4 | Qe7 |

With the sacrificial possibility, ...Nxf2 in mind. Black must resort to tactical sorcery to keep his game alive.

20.   Qxa7

33.

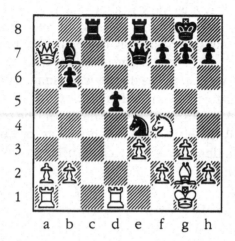

A bold decision requiring very delicate calculations, but a correct one.

20.   ...   Nxf2!

If he tries to preface this sacrifice with 20...d4 to open the diagonal, there comes 21...exd4 Nxf2 22. Re1! and Black is left with hanging pieces, an undesirable alternative to hanging Pawns.

21.   Nxd5!

21. Kxf2 would lose to 21...Qxe3+ 22. Kf1 Rc2.

21.   ...   Bxd5
22.   Qxe7   Nxd1!

The best chance. After 22...Rxe7 23. Rxd5 White has a winning endgame, not so much in view of his extra Pawn which is rather sick, but because of his 2-1 Pawn majority on the Queenside and his powerful Bishop.

23. Rc1!

Prettily exploiting the back rank weakness to get his last piece into play with tempo. The quaint point is that this move is only possible because of the Knight on d1 which prevents the Rook being taken with check.

23.	...	Rb8
24.	Qb4	Bxg2
25.	Kxg2	Nxe3+
26.	Kg1	

And White eventually converted his material advantage into a win: **26...Re6 27. Qf4 Rd8 28. Qd4 Rde8 29. Qd7 Ng4 30. Rc8 Nf6 31. Rxe8+ Rxe8 32. Qb7 Re6 33. Qb8+ Ne8 34. a4 g6 35. b4 Kg7 36. Qb7 h5 37. Kg2 Kf6 38. h3 Rd6 39. a5 bxa5 40. bxa5 Re6 41. a6 Nc7 42. a7 Re7 43. Qc6+Ke5 44. Kf3** Resigns.

4. Open Files

'Put your Rooks on open files' is a piece of advice every beginner receives, and a very sound piece of advice it is. But like all pieces of sound advice, it can prove to be inadequate, or worse.

34.

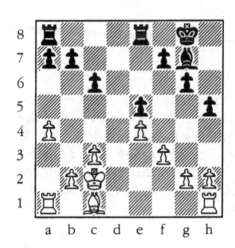

Look at Diagram 34. An innocent-looking position, but if Black (to move) dutifully seizes the only open file with 1...**Rad8** he quickly runs into trouble after 2. **Be3**:

(i) 2...**a6** 3. **Bb6 Rd7** 4. **Rhd1 Ree7** (or 4...Rde7 5. Bd8! Re6 6. Rd7 with decisive penetration) **5. Bc5 Rxd1 6. Rxd1** and the White Rook reaches the seventh rank (6...Rc7?? 7. Rd8+ Kh7 8. Bd6 wins the Rook!).

(ii) 2...**b6** (to prevent the Bishop driving Black off the d file) 3. **a5! c5** (forced) 4. **axb6 axb6** 5. **Ra7** followed by Rha1 with a winning position, e.g. 5...Ra8 6. **Rha1 Rxa7 7. Rxa7 Re6** 8. **Rb7 and Kb3-c4-b5** mopping up the Queenside Pawns.

Why the storm from a clear sky? Because files do not always operate on the first come, first served system. If you look back at variation (i) you will see that Black ran into trouble on the d file, despite having first option on it. So where did he go wrong? Firstly, he failed to appreciate the disparity in strength between the Bishops. The White Bishop was able in variation (i) to drive the Black Rooks off the d file singlehandedly, and in variation (ii) enabled White to open the a file for his own Rooks. In both cases the Black Bishop was a spectator. And secondly, Black had no reason to occupy the d file anyway. Occupation of an open file is of no value unless there is a chance of penetration. Here the White King prevents any possible insurgence on the d file. In particular the entry square on the seventh rank, invariably the most important, is also guarded by the White Bishop, making the d file an entirely prospectless avenue for Black. If the Black King were on, say, e6 rather than g8, the d file would be just as worthless for White.

Returning to the diagram, the correct treatment by Black is **1...Kh7!**, preparing to trade off White's dangerous Bishop, and after **2. Rd1** (threatening of course Rd7) **2...Red8** (not 2...Rad8? 3. Be3 gaining a tempo by the attack on the a Pawn) **3. Be3 Bh6!**, because the Pawn-grabbing attempt 4. Rxd8 Rxd8 5. Bxa7 allows Black in on the seventh rank (5...Rd2+). Better is **4. Bc5** threatening to seize control of the file with Be7, but Black can defend with **4...Bg5** to be followed by bringing his King across to e6. (However, after 5. g3 [threatening 6. h4] 5...h4 [forced] 6. Bd6! will either win the e Pawn or allow White to establish a Rook on the 7th rank after 6...Bf6 7. Bc7, when Black is still in serious difficulties. Also, if 6...Re8 7. Bc7! Re7? 8. Bd8 wins.—*editor*) It must be stressed that open files only have value as a means of feeding Rooks (or possible Queens) into the enemy position, so that a file has no value unless there is somewhere along it an entry point, i.e. an advanced point on which a Rook can safely land. The ideal entry point is on the seventh rank or the second rank (i.e. d7 or d2 on the d file, etc.). Every Rook secretly dreams of landing on the seventh or second ranks, making a 90-degree right (or left) turn and eating its way through the enemy lines. There is something magical about the number seven for a White Rook. Alternatively, points of entry on the eighth, sixth, or even fifth rank can be just as effective. But there must be one, otherwise the file is useless. In this respect the King can play an important role. In the endgame, there is no piece better equipped to defend entry points than the King. For example, a King on e2 simultaneously covers three entry squares on the d file (d1, d2 and d3), a feat which no other piece (apart from the Queen of course) can perform. This makes the location of the opposing King a vital factor in assessing the value of an open file in the endgame. The basic rule is the further from the King, the better. Returning to our example, we can see that the d file was not a useful commodity for Black because of the proximity of the White King, yet the very same file was potentially lethal in White's hands as the Black King was far away.

We can see this principle operating in the following variation of the Sicilian Defense, the so-called Maroczy Bind: **1. e4 c5 2. Nf3 Nc6 3. d4 cxd4 4. Nxd4 g6 5. c4 Nf6 6. Nc3 Nxd4 7. Qxd4 d6 8. Be3 Bg7 9. f3 0-0 10. Qd2 Be6 11. Rc1 Qa5 12. Nd5 Qxd2+ 13 Kxd2.**

35.

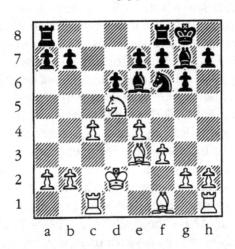

Theory assesses this position as very favorable for White. Why? Because the c file is going to be opened and the White King is much closer than the Black one. As a result White is able to take control.

13.   ...   Bxd5

There is no choice but to take the Knight, and 13...Nxd5 14. cxd5 Bd7 15. Rc7 is immediately decisive, so the text move is forced.

14.   cxd5   Rfc8

Everything seems okay with Black, as 15. Rxc8+ Rxc8 16. Bxa7 achieves nothing in view of 16...Ra8 regaining the Pawn at once, but the favorable position of the White King presents him with other possibilities.

15.   Rxc8+Rxc8
16.   g3!

36.

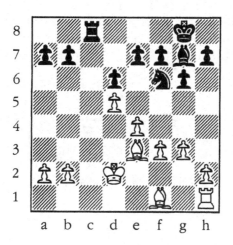

The key move. White intends to drive the enemy Rook off the file with Bh3. He is only able to employ this strategy of conceding the open file, then playing to regain it, because the Black Rook has no point of entry.

Let us analyze the position a little to see just how serious the threat of Bh3 can be:

(i) **16...Kf8** (bringing the King across to bolster the

Queenside) **17. Bh3 Rc4 18. b3 Rc7 19. Bxa7.** White has won a Pawn for nothing (19...Bh6+ 20. Kd3).

(ii) **16...a6** (to keep the Pawn out of harm's way) **17. Bh3 Rc7 18. Rc1!** (Simple chess. The idea is to win a Pawn with Bc8) **18...Ne8** (or 18...Rxc1 19. Kxc1 b5 20. b4! and 21. Bc8) **19. b3 Bb2 20. Rxc7 Nxc7 21. Bc8 b5 22. Bb6** winning at least one Pawn.

(iii) **16...Nd7 17. Bh3 Rc7 18. Bxd7! Rxd7 19. b3 a6 20. Rc1.** Winning the file and probably the game as well.

Although this does not exhaust Black's defensive possibilities, it does show that he has problems to solve. These problems arise primarily out of his inability to contest White's h3-c8 diagonal and the consequent difficulty in holding on to the c file.

The minor pieces play a major role in determining who controls open files. The side with the more active minor pieces can generally count on gaining access to any files that may open up. This is basically what happened in our previous examples. Naturally, outposts too have their part to play. This is better illustrated by Diagram 37 than by words alone.

37.

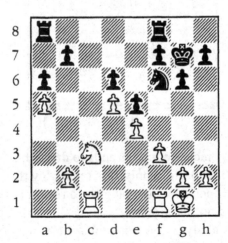

The main features of the position are an open c file and a White outpost on b6. The latter enables White to win the file in a very straightforward manner: 1. Na4 Rac8 2. Nb6 Rxc1 3. Rxc1 Rb8 (what else?) 4. Rc7 Ne8 (what else?) 5. Rd7 and Black has been totally run out of moves. The winning process for White is to centralize his King and then win the d Pawn with Nc4. In the meantime Black has only waiting moves at his disposal.

Chess is very much a team game. The pieces rely heavily on each other's help and cooperation, so if one does not pull its weight it lets the whole side down. If you look back you will see that in no example so far has one side lost out on a file because his Rooks were badly placed. In each case the team has been dragged down by the inability of some Bishop or Knight to match its opposite number. There is an old chess maxim: 'If one piece is bad, the whole position is bad.' How true. Maybe this will explain why there is so much talk of Bishops, Knights and Kings (alas no cabbages!) in a chapter on open files.

38.

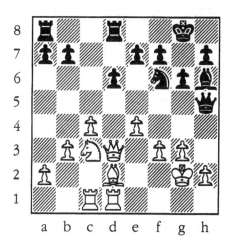

There are, however, times when the major pieces have the right to determine their own destinies, and in these cases the first come, first served principle does operate. Diagram 38 shows a position structurally similar to a previous example of ours, but the presence of Queens adds a new dimension.

1.   Nd5

As before White uses this move to force open the c file, but this time simply because his heavy pieces are much better placed to contest the file than his opponent's. In particular, the Black Queen is horribly out of play on h5.

1.   ...   Nxd5

Again there is little choice in the matter. The White Knight is too strong to be allowed to stay on the board.

2.   cxd5 Rac8
3.   Rc3!

Ensuring control of the file. The bleak position of the Black Queen means that White can dominate through sheer weight of numbers.

3.   ...   Bxd2
4.   Rxd2 Qh6

Scuttling back into play, but the file is already lost.

5.   Rdc2 Qf8
6.   a4

Superfluous. The immediate Rc7 is called for.

6.   ...   Qe8
7.   Rc7! Rxc7
8.   Rxc7 Rb8

The power of a Rook on the seventh rank. It ties down both the Black major pieces single-handed.

9.   Qc3

A multi-purpose move. White consolidates his grip on the file, at the same time threatening Qb4 which stretches Black's defenses to the limit.

9.   ...   Qd8
10.   e5

Opening new avenues of attack. White can afford the luxury of this aggressive, but weakening move only because the opposing forces are totally immobilized.

10.   ...   a6

Preparing to open some lines for his own pieces with ...b5. If Black could ever break out of his strait-jacket, White's King would be a sitting duck.

11.   h4!

With h5 and h6 in mind. Black lacks the manpower to defend both his Pawns and his King.

11.   ...   b5
12.   Rc6

Seizing upon the negative aspect of Black's quest for freedom, White gains the use of the c6 square as an outpost.

12.   ...   bxa4
13.   bxa4   dxe5
14.   Qxe5   Rc8

The a Pawn is taboo. 15. Rxa6? Rc2+ 16. Kh3 Qc8+. As already remarked, White must keep a firm grip on the position because his King is potentially vulnerable.

15.   g4!

Turning the vague possibility of h5 and h6 into reality.

Notice White's use of c6 as an outpost. Black dare not trade Rooks because the resulting passed Pawn would soon Queen. As a result the White Rook can enjoy permanent residence there without fear of removal or exchange.

15.   ...   e6

39.

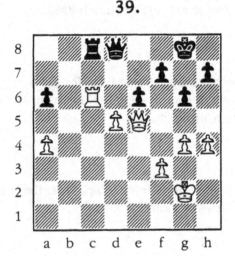

A desperate try to undermine the Rook. He otherwise lacks a good defense to h5 and h6.

16.   Qc3!   Rxc6

Equivalent to resignation, but there is no alternative. 16...Rb8 17. dxe6 fxe6 18. Rc7 leads to mate or win of Queen.

17.   dxc6   Kf8??

And now a simple blunder, but after the forced

17...Qc7 18. a5 (threatening Qc5 followed by Qb6) Kf8 19. Qb4+ Ke8 20. Qb7! Kd8 (20...Qxa5 21. c7 Qd2+ 22. Kh3) 21. Qxa6, White must win.

18. c7 Qc8
19. Qh8+ and Black resigned.

One of the dangers of falling behind in development in the opening is that the enemy Rooks will be first on the scene and will take possession of the open files before your own can be scrambled into action. Rooks are notoriously difficult to bring into play quickly, so any loss of time incurred early on is liable to postpone their development still further. Many games have been won or lost because of this, but few display this motif with subtlety of the following encounter.

White: U. Andersson, Black: R. Knaak
Capablanca Memorial Tournament, 1974

1. Nf3 Nf6 2. c4 b6 3. g3 Bb7 4. Bg2 c5 5. 0-0 g6 6. b3 Bg7 7. Bb2 0-0 8. Nc3 Ne4 9. Qc2 Nxc3 10. Bxc3 Bxc3 11. Qxc3 d5?!

40.

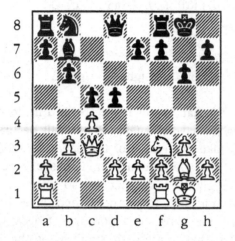

The exchanges initiated by Black's eighth move have left him slightly behind in development. As a result he should try to keep the position closed with 11...d6. White now takes the opportunity to open up the game, which in turn enables him to be first to the central files with his Rooks.

12.	d4!	cxd4
13.	Qxd4	dxc4
14.	Qxc4	Nc6
15.	Rfd1	

In simple near-symmetrical positions the advantage of the move can be considerable. Here Black has problems finding a hideout for his Queen, e.g. 15...Qc7? 16. Nd4 Rac8 17. Bxc6 Bxc6 18. Rac1 Rfd8 19. Nxc6 Rxd1+ 20. Rxd1 Qxc6 21. Rd8+!

15.	...	Qe8
16.	Qf4!	

The strongest and aesthetically most pleasing moves

76

in chess are often very quiet ones. This innocent-looking Queen move suddenly renders Black's position most precarious. With possibilities of an invasion on c7 or h6, Black must tread warily.

16. ...   Rc8

Eliminating one of the threats, while 17. Qh6 can be met by f6. 16...e5 was unfortunately impossible because of 17. Nxe5!

17. Rd2!

Another mouse-like move with the strength of a lion. White doubles on the d file because he can see an entry point on d7.

17. ...   Kg7

Clearly worried about the constant 'threat' of Qh6. The alternative, 17...f6 (threatening e5 and e4), is hardly inviting after 18. Bh3! Rd8 19. Be6+ Kg7 20. Rad1 Rxd2 21. Rxd2 Nd8 22. Nd4.

18. Rad1 Ba8

Finally threatening e5 and e4, but White has a very simple reply.

19. Ne5 Nxe5
20. Qxe5+f6

Or 20...Kg8 also sees White's major pieces penetrating in classic style: 21. Bxa8 Rxa8 22. Rd7 e6 23. Qf6! followed by Re7 and Rdd7.

21. Qe6 Bxg2
22. Rd7!

41.

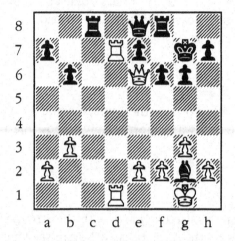

The triumphant entrance! We now see the immense power of a Rook on the seventh row.

22.   ...   Rf7
23.   Kxg2   Rc5

He cannot avoid losing a Pawn. His position after 23...Ra8 24. Rc7 and Rdd7 would be laughable.

24.   Rxa7   b5

An amusing alternative is 24...Re5 25. Qxb6 Rxe2 26. Rd8! checkmating the Queen.

25.   e3

At this point Black acknowledged the hopelessness of his cause by resigning, hardly a premature decision as he has a Pawn less and no constructive moves at all. A possible continuation would be 25...Re5 26. Qb6 (threatening Rd8) Rf8 27. Rdd7 and Qc7.

To summarize, the use of open files can be broken down into three parts:

78

(i) Take control of the file.

(ii) Find a point of entry (this is the important part; without an entry point a file has no value).

(iii) Penetrate via the entry point.

Obviously no steadfast rules can be laid down about what to do after stage (iii). You just have to play it by ear. In the majority of cases, however, the right plan is readily apparent. To round off our discussion of open files, we look at an endgame from Karpov-Uhlmann, Madrid 1973, which exhibits a very common product of open file play, doubled Rooks on the seventh rank.

42.

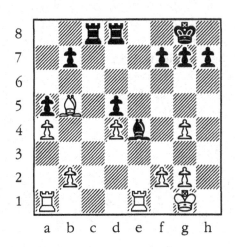

Here White (to move) controls the e file, because of his powerful Bishop outpost on b5. Indeed his entire advantage can be ascribed to the superiority of his minor piece over its opposite number. The Black Bishop has no outpost as it can be driven away from e4.

1.	f3	Bg6
2.	Re7	

The entry point.

2.	...	b6
3.	Rae1	

More accurate than 3. Rb7 Rc2. He gives Black no chance to counter-penetrate by exploiting the back row weakness (3...Rc2?? 4. Re8+).

3.	...	h6
4.	Rb7	Rd6

Passive defense. More competitive but insufficient is 4...Rc2 viz. 5. Ree7 (The b Pawn is not important. What is important is to prise open the seventh rank for his Rooks.) 5...Rxb2 6. Be8 Rc8!(also playing for doubled Rooks on the seventh) 7. Bxf7+ Bxf7 8. Rxf7 Rcc2 9. Rxg7+ Kf8 10 Kh2! (were he to allow his King to be trapped on the back rank, White would be unable to win) 10...Rxg2+ 11. Kh3 and White's King can now escape the checks and his own Rooks triumph, e.g. 11...Rh2+ 12. Kg3 Rhg2+ 13. Kf4 Rb4 14. Rh7! Kg8 (14...Rxd4+ 15. Ke5!) 15. Rhd7 and wins.

5.	Ree7	h5

This time 5...Rc2 loses a Pawn to 6. Rb8+ Kh7 7. Ree8 Rc1+ 8. Kh2 Bb1 (forced to avoid mate) 9. Rh8+ Kg6 10. Rhd8!, e.g. 10...Rxd8 11. Rxd8 Ba2 12. Rd6+.

6.	gxh5	Bxh5
7.	g4	Bg6
8.	f4!	

In order to open the seventh rank for his Rooks, White must drive the Bishop from its defense of f7. The direct 8. Be8 can be met by Rf6.

8.	...	Rc1+
9.	Kf2	Rc2+
10.	Ke3	Be4

He can no longer hold the f7 point—10...Rf6?? 11. f5 Bh7 12. Re8 mate.

11.	Rxf7	Rg6
12.	g5	Kh7

The immediate 12...Rxb2 leads to much the same result after 13. Rfe7 threatening Be8.

13.	Rfe7	Rxb2
14.	Be8	

Clearing the final obstacle to White's total domination of the seventh rank.

14.	...	Rb3+
15.	Ke2	Rb2+
16.	Ke1	Rd6

The checks won't last forever, e.g. 16...Rb1+ 17. Kd2 Rb2+ 18. Kc3 Rc2+ 19. Kb3.

17.	Rxg7+	Kh8
18.	Rge7	Black resigns.

When the checks run out White's mating threats (Rb8 and Bishop moves) are unstoppable.

5. Half-open files: the minority attack

The open file is a double-edged weapon. Although a way to feed the major pieces into the heart of the opponent's position, there is always the danger of it being seized and used to reciprocal effect by the enemy. In short, it is a two-way road for Rooks. The chessplayer, not being an unselfish advocate of equality of opportunity, naturally prefers a one-way system. The half-open file is precisely this. We do not have to go very far (three moves to be exact) to find an example of one: 1. d4 d5 2. c4 e6 3. cxd5 exd5.

43.

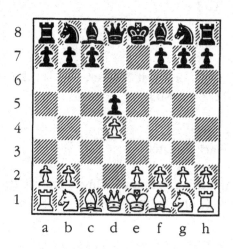

White has the half-open c file, Black the half-open e file. So what does this mean? Cannot Black always erect a granite wall on the c file by c6 and White do similarly on the e file by e3? Yes of course, but the point is that the Black Pawn chain b7, c6, d5 can by challenged by White with b4 and b5. When b5 comes, there is no way Black can avoid being left with a weak Pawn. If he captures away from c6, the d Pawn is left isolated, while allowing an exchange on c6 will leave the c Pawn backward. These are the simple mechanics of the *minority attack*. It is no more nor less than a method of weakening an otherwise sound Pawn set-up by advancing Pawns at it. The process is quite long and slow, the payoff at the end relatively small (one weak Pawn to aim at, two maybe if you are lucky), but its value is undeniable. Moreover, it cannot easily rebound on you. An open file can change hands, a half-open file cannot. Indeed it cannot even be challenged. Imagine the contortions Black would have to go through to oppose Rooks on the c file in front of his Pawns in a position akin to that of Diagram 43. Out of the question. The minority attack has a certain inevitability about it. Though cumbersome, once the mighty wheels have been set in motion, the opposition has no way to apply the brakes.

So much for extolling the virtues of half-open files, but going to Diagram 43 we see that Black has the e file. Surely, he too can launch a minority attack in due course? Not so easy. A minority attack on the e file would involve advancing his f and g Pawns. But where is he to put his King? Certainly not on the Queenside in the path of White's attack. On the other hand it is not the height of expediency to castle Kingside and then send your Kingside Pawns scampering off into the distance to create just one weak Pawn in the enemy camp. The final reward is simply not worth the risk. In general one cannot afford to mount a minority attack in front of a castled King. These attacks only usually work on the other side of the board.

Let us look at a couple of examples of play from Diagram 43 to see how the minority attacks work out in practice.

1. d4 d5 2. c4 e6 3. cxd5 exd5 4. Nc3 Nf6 5. Bg5 Be7 6. e3 c6 7. Qc2 0-0 8. Bd3 Nbd7 9. Nf3 Re8 10. 0-0 Nf8 11. Rab1

44.

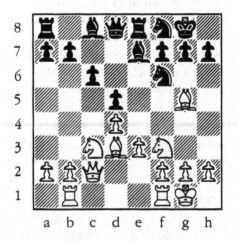

This is a standard position in the so-called (for obvious reasons) Exchange Variation of the Queen's Gambit. White's method of development is both simple and economical, and with his last move he prepares to set the minority attack in motion, by b4. Black's method of play has been a little more contorted (Re8, Nf8), the reason being that not having a worthwhile minority attack of his own, he wants to channel as many pieces as possible over to the Kingside in order to create some diversionary threats there.

Our first example, Van den Berg-Kramer 1950, proceeded:

| 11. | ... | g6 |

So as to play Ne6 without losing a Pawn to Bxf6.

12.	b4	a6
13.	a4	Ne6
14.	Bh4	

No need to rush things with 14. Bxf6 Bxf6 15. b5. In

fact after 15...axb5 16. axb5 c5! 17. dxc5 Nxc5 Black is becoming quite active (he threatens Nxd3 and Bf5).

14.	...	Ng7
15.	b5	axb5
16.	axb5	Bf5

Black's lengthy maneuvers have been designed to exchange this piece, always a problem child in the Queen's Gambit.

| 17. | bxc6 | bxc6 |
| 18. | Ne5 | |

Beginning to harvest the fruits of his Queenside campaign.

| 18. | ... | Rc8 |
| 19. | Rb7 | |

A useful fringe benefit. White has first crack at the newly opened b file. Notice the way his pieces have gained momentum in the wake of the advancing Pawns.

| 19. | ... | Bxd3 |
| 20. | Qxd3 | Rc7 |

White was threatening 21. Bxf6 Bxf6 22. Nxf7.

| 21. | Rxc7 | Qxc7 |
| 22. | Rc1 | |

With the new threat 23. Bxf6 Bxf6 24. Nxd5.

| 22. | ... | Qb7 |
| 23. | Qb1! | Qa6 |

23...Qxb1 24. Nxb1 wins a Pawn.

85

24.	Na2

And White is winning the c Pawn, e.g. 24...Rc8 25.
Bxf6 Bxf6 26. Nb4 etc.

If Black is unable to throw any tactical spanners in the
works, the well-oiled, mechanical minority attack will
generally swallow up a Pawn sooner or later.

Our second example shows how to create counterplay
against the minority attack. Resuming from the position of
Diagram 44:

11.	...	a5
12.	a3	Ne4
13.	Bxe7	Qxe7
14.	b4	axb4
15.	axb4	Ng6
16.	b5	Bg4

45.

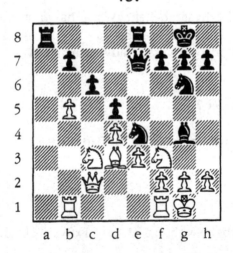

Black is feeding pieces over to the Kingside much
more efficiently than in the previous example. White must
now proceed with caution. On 17. Nd2?, there comes
17...Nxd2 18. Qxd2 Nh4! The powerful threats 19...Bh3! and

19...Bf3! leave White at a loss for a reasonable reply, e.g. 19. f3 Qxe3+! 20. Qxe3 Rxe3 21. fxg4 Rxd3.

Even here, however, White can extract something from the position by judicious play, i.e. 17. Bxe4! dxe4 18. Nd2 Bf5 19. bxc6 bxc6 20. Ne2 with threats of Qxc6 or Ng3. The two Knights do a good job here, hopping in and out of the weak squares created by White's Queenside advance. The minority attack is not purely geared to producing weak Pawns, but creates outposts as well (c5 in this case).

Given that a minority attack runs more smoothly away from the central files (we saw in our previous examples that White could operate a minority attack with some effect on the c file, whereas Black found it difficult to get going on the e file), and the startling criterion that a Pawn minority is needed for a minority attack, it is not difficult to appreciate that the best place to acquire a Pawn majority is in the center. A surplus of Pawns in the middle necessarily means a deficit somewhere else (assuming of course both sides do have equal Pawns). Remember the old rule 'always capture towards the center' applying to a choice of Pawn captures. The advantage of the central Pawn majority is the *raison d'etre* for this piece of advice. The hidden implication is: accumulate Pawns in the center and you can start minority attacks on the flanks.

Take the following variation of the English Opening: **1. c4 Nf6 2. Nc3 d5 3. cxd5 Nxd5 4. g3 g6 5. Bg2 Nxc3 6. bxc3 Bg7.**

46.

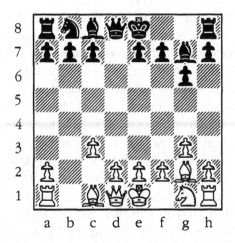

By recapturing the Knight 'towards the center' (i.e. with the b Pawn rather than the d Pawn), White has given himself an extra central Pawn. The offshoot of this is a half-open b file which can later on in the game be used for a minority attack. To this end he does well to adopt a solid but purely passive Pawn set-up in the center (say Pawns on e2, d3, c4) so as to be able to direct all his fire-power to the left flank later on. Diagram 47 shows the type of position that might occur later on after some exchanges. White is ready to launch his minority attack.

47.

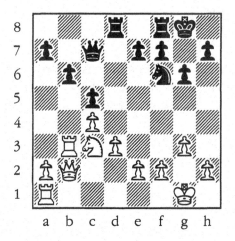

1.   a4   e6

Black wants to hold his Queenside together by Nd7 without allowing a White Knight to jump into d5.

2.   a5   Nd7

Taking the a Pawn would split up Black's Pawns too much, e.g. 2...bxa5? 3. Nb5 Qe7 4. Rxa5 and the other a Pawn will not last long either.

3.   axb6   axb6
4.   Rba3

With an obvious invasion threat on the seventh rank. Despite only having one file and one weakness to work on, White can make life very uncomfortable for his opposite number.

4.   ...   Qc6

The passive 4...Rb8 5. Ra7 Rb7 is hopeless viz. 6. Nb5 Qb8 7. Rxb7 Qxb7 8. Ra7 Qc8 9. Nd6 Qd8 10. Rb7 followed by

Qb5 will win the b Pawn with the prospect of more to come.

5.	Ra7	Ra8
6.	Ne4	

The tremor of White's queenside activity is gradually beginning to be felt right across the board. The immediate threat is 7. Rxd7! followed by Nf6+. It is very interesting the way a single weakness can spread disease throughout the entire position (as a result of one backward Pawn on b6, Black now finds his King under direct threat).

6.	...	Rxa7

Against the immediate 6...f5, White can win a Pawn as follows: 7. Rxa8 Rxa8 8. Rxa8+ Qxa8 9. Qb5 fxe4 (9...Qd8? 10. Qxd7!) 10. Qxd7 Qa1+ 11. Kg2 Qe5 12. Qd8+Kg7 13. Qxb6.

7.	Rxa7	f5

The Knight must be dislodged. 7...Ra8 8. Rxa8+ Qxa8 9. Qb5 sees Black going down without a fight (9...Qd8? 10. Qxd7!).

8.	Ng5	h6
9.	Qb5!	Qxb5
10.	cxb5	hxg5
11.	Rxd7	

The dust clears leaving White with a superactive Rook which should lead to the win of at least a Pawn in the ensuing endgame, e.g. 11...Ra8 12. Rd6 or 11...Rb8 12. Re7.

So what part, if any, does the central Pawn majority play in the minority attack? A considerable part. The plan of seeping into the Black position via the Queenside is essentially slow and nonforcing. It only succeeds because Black has no point to counterattack, and this in turn is due to the impervious White center. Minority attacks must be built on the foundation of a firm central position. The victory may be won on the flank, but ultimately it is created in the center.

Minority attacks derive from the Pawn structure, Pawn structures derive from the opening. Go back to the eras of Capablanca and Alekhine and you will see Queen's Gambits, hoards of them, with hoards of minority attacks descending from them. Nowadays* the Sicilian Defense is all the rage. Sicilians here, Sicilians there, Sicilians absolutely everywhere. Why this saturation with Sicilians? Does the Mafia's influence really extend this far? The answer lies in the minority attack. The whole idea of the Sicilian is for Black to trade his c Pawn for the d Pawn. White almost invariably obliges: 1. e4 c5 2. Nf3 Nc6 (or d6 or e6 or g6) 3. d4 cxd4, when Black immediately arrives at a minority attack Pawn structure. Half-open c file, extra central Pawn, 2-3 minority on the Queenside; these are all the necessary ingredients. Sounds infallible, so where's the snag? Why doesn't Black win every game? The problem is of course that White has a lead in development in the early stages, which may prove difficult to survive. Black's prospects lie later in the game when the winds of White's initiative have blown themselves out.

White: L. Vogt, Black: U. Andersson
Havana 1975

1. e4 c5 2. Nf3 d6 3. d4 cxd4 4. Nxd4 Nf6 5. Nc3 e6 6. Be2 a6 7. f4 Qc7 8. 0-0 Be7 9. Kh1 Nc6 10. Be3 Nxd4 11. Qxd4 0-0 12. Rad1 b5

*Written in 1978. By 2002 little has changed.

48.

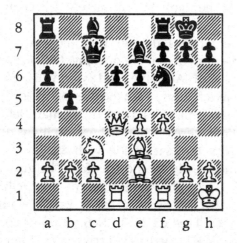

A fairly typical Sicilian position. White has more space and better development, but Black is solidly placed. His last move does give a hint of the minority attack one day to come, but his primary concern for the moment is to complete his development before a tactical accident befalls him.

13. e5

Trying to precipitate an accident.

13. ... dxe5
14. Qxe5

A devious attempt to exploit Black's lag in development. The idea lies in 14...Qxe5 15. fxe5 Nd7 16. Bf3 Rb8 17. Ba7 slaying the Rook in its bed. However, Black has an equally devious response up his sleeve.

14. ... Qb8!

She who turns and runs away saves her Rook for later play. Now 15. Bf3 can be simply met by Bb7.

15.   Qxb8

White suddenly finds his box of tricks empty and so submits to an exchange of Queens, but the endgame gives Black an excellent opportunity to play his minority attack.

15.   ...   Rxb8
16.   Ba7   Ra8
17.   Bb6   Bb7
18.   a3   Rfc8!

A good time to compare the relative values of open and half-open files. White has the d file (his Bishop on b6 sees to that), but no entry point, no threats, no pressure. Black has the half-open c file. He threatens ...Bxa3, undermining the Knight. The Knight cannot move away because it is 'pinned' in front of the c Pawn. Half-open files do not need entry points. They naturally generate pressure.

19.   Ba5

Bolstering the threatened Knight.

19.   ...   g6

A useful little move. White's Pawn on f4 is something of a liability and Black intends to keep it there as such.

20.   h3?

The psychological effect of a waiting move pays immediate dividends. As in trench warfare, the worst part of defending against a minority attack is waiting for it to come. White wants to free his back rank from possible threats later on, but in doing so weakens his Kingside Pawns too much. Better is 20. Bb4.

20.	...	h5!

Heading for h4 to isolate the weak White f Pawn from the g Pawn. This advance ensures that Black will have targets on both sides of the board to aim at.

21.	Bf3	Bxf3
22.	Rxf3	h4!
23.	Rd2	Rc4

49.

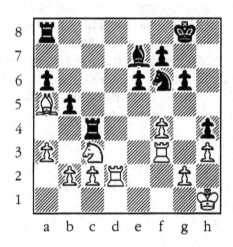

Showing yet another feature of the half-open file, the outpost on c4. Not an outpost in the strict sense of the word as White can drive the Rook away, but only at the cost of severely weakening his defenses on the c file.

24.	b3

Undesirable, but forced. There is no other way to counter the plan of ...Rac8 (pinning the Knight in front of the c Pawn) and ...Nh5 winning the f Pawn . Notice the way Black uses a Pawn weakness on the Kingside (f4) to engineer a weakening of the Queenside (b3).

24.	...	Rc6
25.	a4	b4
26.	Ne2	Rac8

The minority attack has done its job. White is left with a backward c Pawn.

27. c4

This solves his problems on the c file only to create a fresh weakness on the b file. The logical way to defend is to try and trade Rooks by 27. Nd4 Rc3 28. Rxc3 Rxc3 29. Rd3 Rxd3 30. cxd3, but even this fails to save White as his Pawns are too split, viz. 30...Nd5 31. Ne2 Kg7, and if 32. Kg1 Bc5+ 33. d4 (or 33. Kf1 Ne3+!) 33...Bd6 when White cannot bring his King to f3 because of 34. Kf2 Bxf4 35. Nxf4 Nxf4 36. Bxb4? Nd3+.

27.	...	bxc3 e.p.
28.	Rxc3	Nd5
29.	Rxc6	Rxc6

50.

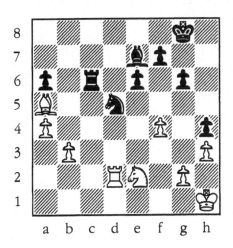

The beginning of a new phase. White has two weaknesses (f4, b3), one as a result of the minority attack, one as a result of his own ineptitude (20. h3?). Black's task is now to attack each in turn and thereby completely tie down the White forces. There is no counterplay to reckon with, the dominating Knight sees to that.

30.   Rb2

A doomed attempt to straighten his Queenside out with b4.

30.   ...   Bf6
31.   Ra2   Rc8

To transfer to the b file. Although it may appear that Black had a faster winning combination with 31...Nxf4 (?) 32. Nxf4 Re1+ 33. Kh2 Be5 34. Bd2 Rd1, with the twin threats of ...Rxd2 and ...g5, this concept is flawed because of 35. g3! hxg3 36. Kg2. Andersson's method is correct.

32.   Bd2   Rb8
33.   Nc1   Nb4
34.   Bxb4   Rxb4

The outpost in front of the backward Pawn.

35.   Rf2   Be7
36.   Rf3   Bd6
37.   Ne2

Everything miraculously still defended, but White is reduced to total passivity.

37.   ...   Re4
38.   Rd3

Again the only way to avoid immediate material loss (38. Rf2 Bc5).

38.	...	Bc5
39.	Rc3	Bf2
40.	Rc2	Kg7

The time is ripe for the King to march in. All the White pieces are amusingly trapped, like a bicycle wheel in a tramline, only able to go backwards and forwards.

41. Ng1

Rather than submit to the humiliation of idling his King to and fro while the Black monarch strides in and mops up. White surrenders a Pawn to free his pieces, but to no avail of course.

41. ... Rxf4 and Black soon won.

The Pawn structure, or rather distribution in this endgame, is well worth remembering. Black had a 4-3 majority on the King side (e, f, g, h Pawns, *vs.* f, g, h Pawns) and White a 3-2 surplus on the Queenside (c, b, a Pawns *vs.* b and a Pawns). This distribution is fundamentally favorable for Black, firstly because of his first extra central Pawn (which in the game provided him with a powerful outpost on d5 for his Knight), and secondly because of the Queenside minority attack. There is also a third advantage not apparent from our last game: four Pawns protect a King better than three. How many times have you read that Black's classical freeing move in the Sicilian is ...d5 without understanding why? If Black can swap his d Pawn for White's e Pawn he reaches the 4-3 *vs.* 2-3 distribution advertised above. Of course, if White can meet ...d5 with e5, it's a different story...

The Sicilian is not the only opening geared to reach this Pawn distribution. For example, the following line of the Caro-Kann 1. e4 c6 2. d4 d5 3. Nc3 dxe4 4. Nxe4 Nd7 5. Bc4 Ngf6 6. Ng5 e6 7. Qe2 Nb6 8. Bd3 h6 9. N(5)f3 c5 sees Black liquidating the White d Pawn to achieve the desired

Pawn set-up. Similarly in the French Defense after 1. e4 e6
2. d4 d5 3. Nc3 dxe4 4. Nxe4 Nd7 5. Nf3 Ngf6, Black soon gets
in c5. These openings have failed to supersede the Sicilian in
popularity only because they are more difficult to handle.*
Although Black obtains the Pawn formation he wants much
faster, he can experience great difficulties in developing his
Queenside. This is always the price paid for freeing your
game too quickly in these openings. If Black can, however,
succeed in bringing all his pieces into play unscarred he is
assured of an equal game—at least. The struggle to develop can
lead to very sharp play.

White: M. Stean, Black: A.J. Mestel
**1. e4 e6 2. d4 d5 3. Nd2 c5 4. exd5 Qxd5 5. Ngf3 cxd4
6. Bc4 Qd6 7. 0-0 Nc6 8. Nb3 Nf6 9. Nbxd4 Nxd4 10
Nxd4 Bd7 11. Bb3 Qc7**

A now familiar Pawn set-up, but Black's many Queen
moves have left him dangerously behind in development. His
last move however prepares ...Bd6 bringing a piece into play
with tempo. If he can safely castle, Black will stand well.

*Interestingly enough, during the twenty or so years since the original text was
written such variations of the Caro-Kann and French have increased in
popularity.

12.   Bg5

Crossing Black's plans. 12...Bd6 is met by 13. Bxf6 gxf6 (13...Bxh2+ 14. Kh1 gxf6 15. g3 wins a piece) 14. Qh5 and the Black King has no safe haven.

12.   ...   Ne4

A bold reply. The quiet 12...Be7 fails to solve all the problems in view of 13. Re1 0-0 14. Nf5!

13.   Bh4   Bd6
14.   Qg4!?

Striving hard to keep the initiative. The more conservative 14. Nf3 0-0 15. Re1 Nc5 allows Black the type of position he is aiming for.

14.   ...   Bxh2+
15.   Kh1   Qf4!
16.   Qxg7

The only consistent continuation, but it runs the gauntlet of Black's dangerous attack.

16.   ...   Qxh4
17.   Qxh8+   Ke7

Threatens both mate and the Queen. Maybe White has overplayed his hand?

18.   Nf3!

Temporary salvation at least.

18.   ...   Qh6

The startling 18...Qxf2 works after 19. Rxf2 Nxf2+

20. Kxh2 Rxh8, but after the simple 19. Qxa8 Black has amazingly enough no mate.

19.   Qxa8

52.

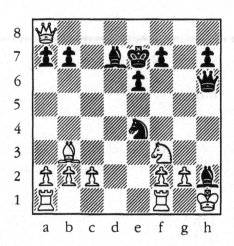

Into the valley of death, or so it seems. But where is the mate? 19...Bd6+ 20. Kg1 Nd2 21. Rfd1! Nxf3+ 22. gxf3 Qh2+ 23. Kf1 Bb5+ 24. c4 and Black has only one more check for his huge material deficit. Could it be that the whole attack is nothing more than an optical illusion and that White has been winning all along?

19.   ...   Ng3+!

Not quite.

20.   fxg3   Bxg3+
21.   Kg1   Qe3+
22.   Kh1   Qh6+ Draw!

An entertaining miniature typical of the modern trend. Complications not for complication's sake, but to preempt the minority attack which would certainly have later come, had Black been given time to consolidate by castling.

The one aspect of the half-open file not properly covered to date is the outpost on the half-open file. This is best explained by an example.

53.

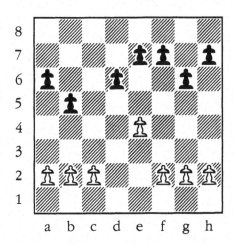

Diagram 53 shows another typical Sicilian Pawn structure. Black has the half-open c file, White the d file. Each has an associated outpost, White on d5, Black on c4. Outpost is something of a misnomer here, for as you may remember an outpost was originally defined as a square that could not be challenged by an enemy Pawn. Here Black can play e6 and White b3 challenging the respective outposts, but only at a cost. b3 weakens the c3 square and so makes the c Pawn more difficult to defend. Correspondingly, e6 weakens the Black d Pawn, so these moves can only be made in exceptional circumstances. The squares d5 and c4 are therefore effectively outposts, if not technically so.

These considerations explain a couple of points about the Sicilian Defense that may have been puzzling you:

(i) Why does Black so often develop his f8 Bishop passively with e6 and Be7 when he can give it a beautiful diagonal by g6 and Bg7? Because e6 and Be7 deprive White of his d5 outpost without leaving the d Pawn too weak. After g6 and Bb7 Black can rarely consider e6 as well.

(ii) Why is the Maroczy Bind (Pawns on e4 and c4) considered so effective for White against the Sicilian? Because with a White Pawn on c4 Black can have no outpost there, and Black can generate very little play on the c file.

Strategical problems are born in the opening, which is why it is so important to *understand* the openings you play. Hopefully this chapter has given you some insight into the workings of the Sicilian Defense and related openings as well as the minority attack.

6. Black squares and White squares

Pawns are quite happy to defend pieces (outposts), yet pieces do not enjoy being tied to the defense of Pawns (weak Pawns). Bear these simple principles in mind and you are well on the way to mastering one of the fundamental problems of chess—cooperation between pieces and Pawns. This harmony between workers and management so to speak is not solely the responsibility of the shop floor. There is no such thing as the 'perfect Pawn formation, because different pieces react in different ways to the same Pawn skeleton. One of the arts of chess strategy is to recognize which of your pieces fit in well with the Pawn structure, and to exchange off the ones that do not. In this context we are referring primarily to minor pieces (i.e. Bishops and Knights).

Recognition of pieces which do or do not fit in well with the Pawn structure centers mainly around the concept of 'good' and 'bad' Bishops. If most of your central Pawns become blocked on Black squares, say, the future for your Black-squared Bishop will be very limited. The White-squared Bishop on the other hand will be completely unimpaired by its Pawns. Moreover, Pawns on Black squares do not protect White squares, so the Bishop is also needed to help cover the 'gaps'. Knights are less likely to be brought up before the Race Relations Board for color consciousness. They are quite happy to hop from Black squares to White and back again.

54.

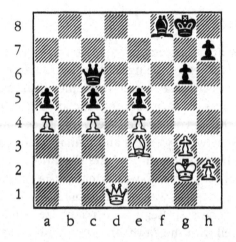

Diagram 54 is a typical case of good Bishop vs. bad Bishop. The Pawn structure is entirely symmetrical, but White's Bishop is compatible with his Pawn structure whereas Black's is a prisoner in his own camp. White wins without effort:

1.	Qd5+	Qxd5
2.	exd5	

He recaptures this way to vacate e4 for his King.

2.	...	Bd6

Black would like to release his Bishop with 2...e4, but the threat of Bd2 (yet another Pawn on a Black square) precludes this.

3.	Kf3	Kf7
4.	Ke4	Kf6
5.	Bd2	Bc7
6.	Bc3	

Not the only way to win. Equally efficient is 6. d6

Bxd6 (6...Bd8 7. Kd5 etc.) 7. Bxa5 any 8. Bc3 any 9. a5 any 10. a6 Bb8 11. Bxe5+! making a new Queen.

| 6. | ... | h6 |

Black has only waiting moves.

| 7. | h3 | h5 |
| 8. | h4 | |

Zugzwang. Any move by Black loses at least a Pawn.

Many people reason 'If I put my Pawns on the same colored squares as my Bishop, I can defend them there'. If you commit *hara-kiri* instead, you won't have to defend them at all. The two solutions are roughly equivalent, give or take the problem of cleaning the blood off the board. The real fallacy in the argument is that if you put all your Pawns on squares of the same color, say Black, there is no defense against enemy penetration on the White squares. Look at Diagram 55.

55.

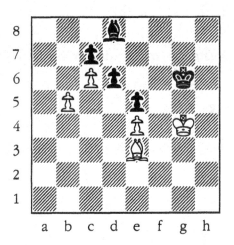

There is only very scanty material left on the board and Black has only one Pawn to keep protected. Yet his

position is hopeless because he cannot prevent the White
King penetrating on the light squares f5, e6, d7:

1.   Bf2! (Amazingly, as pointed out by Mike
Senkiewicz, one of the world's top backgammon players and a
noted chess master, 1. Bg5!! wins on the spot. For if 1...Bxg5
2. b6 and White queens by force. —*editor*)

A quiet move typical of these endgames. White could
win a piece by 1. Ba7 Kf6 2. Bb8 Ke6 3. b6 cxb6 4. c7, but this
only leads to a draw—4...Bxc7 5. Bxc7 d5.

1.   ...   Kg7

Black is forced to give way. Any Bishop move is
answered by 2. b6 cxb6 3. c7, while 1...Kf6?? loses the Bishop
(2. Bh4+).

2.   Kf5   Kf7

The second line of defense.

3.   Be3

Once again forcing a King move in reply, Bishop
moves being met by b6.

3.   ...   Ke7

Or 3...Ke8 4. Ke6 and Black is in zugzwang again.

4.   Bg5+   Ke8
5.   Ke6!!

5. Bxd8 also wins, but the text move is both more
thematic and more aesthetic.

5.   ...   Bxg5

6.   b6

And White gets a new Queen for Christmas: 6...cxb6 7. c7 or 6...Bd8 (or Kd8) 7. b7.

This is what we are talking about when we saw things like '...and Black is weak on the White squares.' We mean there is a danger that a King (in the endgame) or a Queen (in the late middlegame) will be able to penetrate into the position. Using bridge parlance, he has a duplication of honors. His Pawns cover Black squares, his Bishop does the same, so that after suitable exchanges there will be little more than overworked King to guard the other thirty-two.

Naturally the less material on the board, the clearer the bad Bishop syndrome. This is why we started the section with two examples of pure Bishop endgames. With Rooks on as well however the overall strategy is much the same.

56.

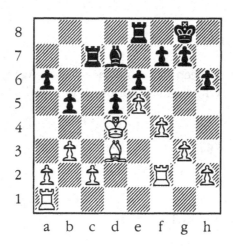

Diagram 56 is an endgame (Tarrasch-Teichmann, San Sebastian, 1912) which all exponents of the French Defense should try to avoid. Black has a bad Bishop and weak Black squares. The execution runs as follows:

1.	g4

The key to the White position is his King's outpost on d4. Because Black has no minor piece able to operate on Black squares, he cannot usurp the White monarch from its throne and moreover must keep a Rook permanently stationed on the c file to prevent his majesty from walking in. You may remember that the 'weakness' of weak Pawns was that pieces could be tied down to their defense. Similarly the 'weakness' of weak squares is that defending pieces must keep them permanently covered to prevent infiltration. To exploit this constraint on the mobility of the Black Rooks, White must bring his own into the game. This he does by a general advance on the Kingside which will eventually lead to the opening of some lines there. He chooses the extreme right flank for this action to stretch the defense as much as possible. In endgames you should try to introduce 'width' into your play, i.e. create trouble on two widely-spaced fronts.

1.	...	Bc8
2.	h4	g6

Trying to keep the Kingside closed. Against purely waiting tactics White would continue Rg1 and g5, meeting ...h5 with g6.

3.	Rh1	Kg7
4.	h5	Rh8

He cannot barricade the Kingside by 4...g5 because of 5. fxg5 hxg5 6. h6+ Kg8 7. Rh5 etc.

5.	Rfh2	Bd7
6.	g5	

Opening the King's wing by force, thus enabling his Rooks to get their teeth into Black's position.

6.	...	hxg5
7.	fxg5	gxh5
8.	Rxh5	Rxh5
9.	Rxh5	

57.

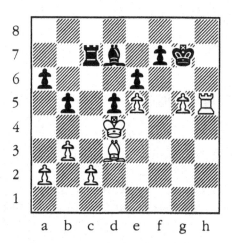

A good point for a brief resume on the state of play. White has secured an open file *plus* an entry point (h7), while the Black Rook is still playing the role of nightwatchman. Initially White had the better Bishop, now he has the better Rook as well.

9.	...	Kf8
10.	Rh8+	Ke7
11.	g6	

Opening up the seventh rank for his Rook.

11.	...	fxg6
12	Bxg6	b4

In principle the right idea—establish Pawns on *Black* squares wherever possible—but here it hardly helps at all.

13.   Rh7+?

A mistake. He should not encourage the Black King to run over to the Queenside where it can relieve the Rook from its jobs of custodian of the Black squares (c5 in particular). Correct is the immediate 13. Bd3 leaving the Black King hemmed in on e7.

13.   ...   Kd8
14.   Bd3?

He still had time to rectify his previous error by 14. Rh8+ and 15. Bd3.

14.   ...   Rc3?

There are good drawing chances after 14...Rc6! (vacating c7 for the King) 15. Rh8+ Kc7 16. Ra8 Kb7.

15.   a3!

The vital difference. Black's a Pawn is drawn forward to a5 where it is indefensible.

15.   ...   a5
16.   Rh8+   Ke7

Or 16...Kc7 17. Ra8 Kb6 18. Ra6+ wins the Pawn anyway.

17.   Ra8

and Black resigned as he is losing a Pawn without any improvement in his position.

The natural corollary to these endgames is that if you have a Bishop of one color, it is imperative to establish Pawns, particularly central Pawns, on squares of the other color. It can make the difference between a win and a loss.

58.

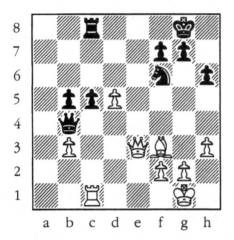

For example, Diagram 58 shows a position from the game Burn-Marshall, Ostend 1907. White (to move) has a strong central passed Pawn, or is it strong? The answer depends on whether or not he can advance it. On d5 it merely obstructs the Bishop, on d6 it is a giant. After the natural 1. d6 c4 2. bxc4 bxc4 3. Qe7 (threat 4. d7!) Re8 4. **Qc7** White has all the chances. Instead, Burn chose the incomprehensible...

1.   Qc3? Qxc3
2.   Rxc3

...allowing his Pawn to be blocked on a White square.

2.   ...   Ne8!

Now Black is clearly in the driving seat. He is effectively at least half a Pawn up, as the White d Pawn is blocked and useless. Moreover the Black squares are weak in as much as White has little to counter the Black King marching to e5.

3.   Kf1   Kf8

111

4.	Be2	Nd6

The ideal square for the Knight. In a sense the White d Pawn 'protects' the Knight from harassment on the d file.

5.	Rc2	Ke7
6.	Ra2	

The only way to activate the Rook is round the back through the tradesman's entrance, but it's very slow.

6.	...	c4
7.	bxc4	bxc4
8.	Ke1	Rc5

Underlining the sad decline in the fortunes of the once proud d Pawn, now a miserable weakness.

9.	Bf3	c3
10.	Kd1	Nb5
11.	Ra4	Kd6
12.	Ra6+	Ke5
13.	Kc1	

A better chance is 13. Rc6 using his outpost, the one remaining value of the passed Pawn. After 13...Kd4! however, White is still in difficulties:

(i) 14. Kc2 Na3+ 15. Kc1 Rb5!

(ii) 14. Rxc5 Kxc5 15. Kc2 Nd4+! 16. Kxc3 Nxf3 17. gxf3 Kxd5 and White loses the King and Pawn endgame because of his broken Pawns viz. 17. Kd3 Ke5 18. Ke3 g5! zugswang.

13.	...	Nd4
14.	d6	

A Black square at last—but too late.

14.   ...   c2
15.   Ra3   Rb5 and Black wins by force viz. 16. Rc3 Rb1+
17. Kd2 Kxd6 18. Be4 c1/Q+ 19 Rxc1 Nb3+!.

The most powerful piece in any endgame is the King,
and the White square/Black square strategy is aimed to carve
out a route into the enemy camp for it. You can see the reason
for stationing Pawns on squares of color opposite to that of
your Bishop by the following little exercise. Set up a White
Bishop on e4 and Pawn on d4 opposed by a Black King on d6.
The King wants to cross the fifth rank. To do so, it must
traverse as far as the g file in one direction (Ke6, f6, g5) or the
a file in the other direcion (Kc7, b6 at which point White can
transfer the Bishop to d3, but now Ka5). Thus we see that a
White-squared Bishop in conjunction with a Black-squared
Pawn provides a pretty wide barrier against an enemy King.
Now transfer the Pawn on d4 to a White square, any White
square (e.g. d5, c4, d3), and the King walks straight through.
So in assessing how bad a bad Bishop is, or equivalently how
weak a weak square complex is with a view to the endgame,
the main criterion must be: how easily can the opponent's
King break in? Let us look at an exceptional example (Diagram
59).

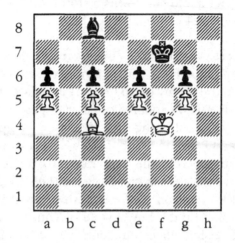

Black has the worst Bishop the world has ever seen and four sick Pawns to defend, yet he cannot lose! Why not? Because the White King can never enter. White can only attack various Pawns with his Bishop, at most two at a time, but the threats are easily parried. Without a King there is no way to win. Now remove the White Pawn from e5. Despite now being a Pawn down, White wins easily because his King can play its part:

1.	Ke5	Ke7
2.	Bd3	Kf7
3.	Kd6	

The Black squares!

3.	...	Bb7
4.	Kc7	Ba8
5.	Kb8	wins everything.

As a final example to emphasize the power of the King in the ending, we turn to one of Tal's early games, against Lisitsin in the 1956 Soviet Championship.

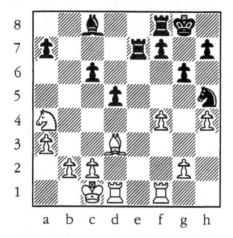

60

In Diagram 60, Tal (White, to move) has all sorts of problems to solve with his ragged Kingside Pawns, but his opponent has some Black square holes in the center. The only way to play such endgames is to exploit your own advantages as vigorously as possible, even if it means total capitulation elsewhere. Here Tal decides to abandon his Kingside to avoid being drawn into passive defense and concentrate all his efforts on the weak Black squares.

1. f5!

Naturally he chooses the most uncooperative method of surrendering the Kingside.

1. ... gxf5

Winning a Pawn, but compromising his Pawn structure to do so. He should instead be willing to fathom the murky depths of 1...Ng3 2. f6! Re6 3. Rf3 Ne4.

2. Rfe1 Rfe8
3. Rxe7 Rxe7
4. Kd2!

The beginning of the royal tour. Naturally the full consequences of such an adventure are not calculable, but calculation is not needed. Have faith in your King.

4.	...	Ng3
5.	Kc3	f4
6.	Kd4	Bf5

To create an entry point on e2 for his Rook. Black has a Pawn more and his pieces are very active, but he is playing without his King.

7.	Rd2	Re6

Or 7...Bxd3 8. cxd3 Re2 9. Rxe2 Nxe2+ 10. Kc5 mopping up in the center.

8.	Nc5	Rh6
9.	Ke5!	

The h Pawn is going too, but no matter. The important point is that Black has no *passed* Pawn to deflect the invading monarch.

9.	...	Bxd3
10.	cxd3	Rxh4
11.	Kd6	Rh6+
12.	Kc7	Nf5
13.	Kb7	

Threatening to promote his a Pawn no less!

13	...	Nd4
14.	Rf2	

Denying Black the chance to make any passed pawns by ...f3. (If 14. Kxa7? Rh2!, threatening 15...f3, causes White problems. —*editor*)

14.	...	a5
15.	Rxf4	Ne6
16.	Rg4+	Kf8
17.	Kxc6	

His majesty now has the audacity to walk into a discovered check. This is in fact the beginning of the end. White has recovered all his material and still has much the more active King.

17.	...	Nxc5+
18.	Kxc5	Re6
19.	Kxd5 and the rest is technique:	

19...Rb6 20. b4 axb4 21. axb4 Ke7 22. Kc5 Rf6 23. Rd4 Rf5+ 24. Kb6 Rf6+ 25. Kc7 Rf5 26. Re4+ Kf6 27. Kc6 Rf2 28. g4 h5 29. gxh5 Kg5 30. b5 f5 31. Rb4 f4 32. b6 f3 33. b7 Black resigns.

Before the endgame God made the middlegame and an opening to lead into it. Here the seeds of these color strategies are sown. As soon as the central Pawn set-ups crystallize into some sort of permanent structure, the respective good and bad Bishops become self-evident. For example, the French Defense usually creates the Pawn centers d4, e5 (White) *v.* d5, e6 (Black) in which cases each side has a 'bad' Queen Bishop. Hence the opening variations: 1. e4 e6 2. d4 d5 3. Nc3 Nf6 4. Bg5 Be7 5. e5 Nfd7 6. Bxe7 trading his bad Bishop for Black's good one: or 1. e4 e6 2. d4 d5 3. Nc3 Bb4 4. e5 b6 preparing Ba6. Here Black is willing to meet 5. Qg4 by ...Bf8, losing two tempi to secure the exchange of his bad Bishop without giving up the good one (i.e. the King Bishop); another idea is 1. e4 e6 2. d4 d5 3. e5 c5 4. c3 Qb6 5. Nf3 Bd7 followed by ...Bb5. Black's idea is always a White square strategy, i.e. exchange his Queen Bishop for the opposing King Bishop and later infiltrate on the White square. White's plan is the exact opposite (exchange Black-squared Bishops and come in on the Black squares). Look back at the Tarrasch-Teichmann ending (Diagram 56). That arose from a French Defense in which White managed to trade Black-squared Bishops early in the game.

To look in some detail at the mechanics of a color strategy in the opening/middlegame we shall turn our attention to the King's Indian Defense. Structurally speaking the K.I.D. is merely a French Defense seen through a mirror, but for some reason or other King's Indian strategy always seems more involved than its reflected counterpart. The following White-square strategy worked out by Petrosian is both subtle and illuminating: **1. d4 Nf6 2. c4 g6 3. Nc3 Bg7 4. e4 d6 5. Be2 0-0 6. Nf3 e5 7. d5** .

61.

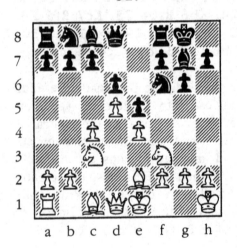

Classically these closed King's Indian positions lead to a race. White plays for c5, Black counters with ...f5 and may the best man win! Petrosian's idea is to maneuver for control of the White squares so as to take the sting out of Black's ...f5 counter *before* launching his own Queenside operations. After all the c5 attack is inherent from the Pawn structure and so will never disappear. Let us see how his idea operates by following a game Petrosian-Yuchtman:

7.   **...**   **Na6** (7...a5 is the standard move here nowadays. —*editor*)

If 7...Ne8 to play ...f5 as quickly as possible, there comes 8. h4 f5 9. h5 opening the h file against Black's castled King position. This is one reason for White closing the center (7. d5) before castling himself.

8.   **Bg5!**

The key move. Superficially the motivation is obvious—Black cannot play ...f5 without moving the Knight and cannot move the Knight without losing his Queen—but the pin is easily broken. Under the surface lies the idea to weaken the White squares.

8.   **...**   **h6**
9.   **Bh4**   **g5**

So what has been achieved? This Bishop has been driven into oblivion and Black is now ready to move ...f5 anyway. But he has made the vital concession ...g5. As every Russian schoolboy knows, when you play ...f5 and White replies exf5, Black must recapture with the g Pawn to prevent White gaining an outpost on e4. Now there is no g Pawn with which to recapture—it has been drawn out of position in pursuit of the Bishop. This means that ...f5 can now never be played without presenting White with a beautiful outpost on e4.

10   **Bg3**   **Nh5**
11.   **Nd2**   **Nf4**

Securing an outpost for himself. White can never contemplate Bxf4 in view of the reply ...exf4! liberating the throttled Bishop. White's whole strategy is to leave Black with a dummy Bishop on g7.

11...Nxg3 12. hxg3 f5 would have played right into

White's hands—13. exf5 Bxf5 14. Nde4 and 15. Bg4. White would later castle Queenside and launch a direct mating attack based on the White squares and the h file.

12.   0-0   Nc5

Taking the other Bishop would not help Black's cause either: 12... Nxe2+ 13. Qxe2 f5 (13...Nc5 14. b4) 14. exf5 Bxf5 15. Nde4 and White can then start thinking in terms of Rac1, a3, b4 and c5, because there is no counterplay.

13.   Bg4

The exchange of White-squared Bishops is the next logical link in the chain of White's strategy.

13.   ...   a5?

Squandering his only chance which play in 13...Bxg4 14. Qxg4 h5! 15. Qf5 h4, as pointed out by Petrosian. White is then forced to free Black's Bishop from its self-captivity by 15. Bxf4 exf4 and Black can later hold his damaged Kingside together by ...Qf6.

14.   f3!

62.

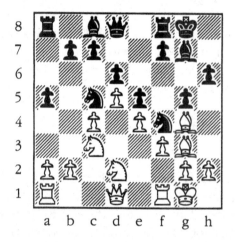

Heralding the successful complication of White's opening strategy. He has completely disarmed Black's Kingside, ...f5 being met by taking and following up with Nde4, while the Bishop on g3 now has a cosy retreat to f2 in the event of ...h5,h4. He can now begin his Queenside build-up with the utmost leisure. The race has been reduced to a one-horse affair—he only has to complete the course to win.

14.   ...   Ncd3

An invasion into thin air, but there is no constructive plan to be found. If 14...Bxg4 15. fxg4 and White gets a super outpost for his Knights on f5.

15.	Qc2	c6
16.	Kh1	h5
17.	Bxc8	Rxc8
18.	a3	cxd5
19.	cxd5	Nc5

There is no way to maintain the Knight on d3, e.g. 19...Qd7 20. Bxf4 Nxf4 21. a4 followed by b3, Nc4, Nb5 etc.

20.	Bf2	g4
21.	g3	Ng6

To put the other Knight on d3 would serve no useful purpose. d3 is not a good outpost for Black—there is no Pawn to support it. The very most a piece can hope for on such an isolated square is survival.

22.	fxg4	hxg4
23.	Be3	

Still no hurry. Black's whole position is built on sand. He has White-square holes but no Bishop to defend them, no capacity to expand or counter-attack. His present position may well be his optimal one, so give him some rope and...

23.	...	b5?

...he might sacrifice a Pawn for nothing.

24.	Nxb5	Qb6
25.	a4	Qa6

Admitting the futility of his 23rd move. The rest is painful. **26. Nc4 f5 27. Rxf5 Rxf5 28. exf5 Qb7 29. Qg2 Nb3 30. Nbxd6 Qd7 31. Rf1** Black resigns.

There are essentially two types of White-square strategy. The first is as above: given a *fixed* Pawn structure in which the enemy Pawns are already on Black squares, you exchange White-squared Bishops with a view to setting up outposts or penetrating on White squares. The second is the same idea back to front: given a more fluid Pawn set-up and that your opponent already has relinquished his White-squared Bishop, you try to draw his Pawns onto Black squares. The objective is the same—to give the opponent a Black-square Pawn formation, with no Bishop to plug the gaps, but the build-up is different.

63.

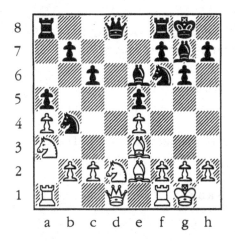

The position in Diagram 63 arose from the opening of the game Stean-Planinc, Moscow 1975. There is as yet no question of bad Bishops or weak squares. Indeed, neither player can reasonably claim to hold the advantage, though White's next move does set one or two problems.

1.   Nac4

With threats to invade on b6 as well as the attack on the e Pawn. Black can now maintain the balance with 1...Nd7, but instead mistakenly resolves to eliminate the annoying Knight.

1.   ...   Bxc4
2.   Bxc4

2. Nxc4 would leave the e Pawn hanging, so why was Black's last move a mistake? Because his Bishop on e6 was a good piece, too good to swap for Knight. If White can now find some way to lure the Black Pawns onto Black squares, he has all the makings of a successful White-square strategy.

| 2. | ... | Qd7 |
| 3. | f3 | |

To prevent the annoying...Ng4 and also bolster the e Pawn in preparation for Bb3 and Nc4.

| 3. | ... | Nh5 |
| 4. | g3 | |

Keeping the Knight out of f4. There is no reason to fear 4...Qh3 in view of 5. Rf2 followed by Bf1 and Nc4.

| 4. | ... | Rad8 |
| 5. | Bb3! | |

64.

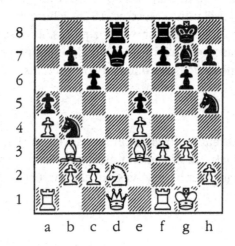

So far White has been defending, but this move marks the turning of the tide. Black has reached the top of the hill and is about to roll all the way down again. Without his White-squared Bishop he has no way of making any further impression on the White position, but instead must meet the threat of 6. Nc4 followed by Bb6 winning the a Pawn. The only way to do so involves the weakening of his White squares.

5.	...	c5
6.	Qe2	

Of course not 6. Bxc5?? Qxd2. White can afford to take things very calmly. His domination of the White squares is probably already a winning advantage.

6.	...	b6
7.	Rfd1	Qc7
8.	c3	Nc6

8...Nd3? loses a piece to 9. Nc4.

9.	Nc4	Nf6
10	Na3	

White has a number of good outposts for his pieces (all on White squares!). The Knight has sniffed out one on b5.

10.	...	Na7
11.	Qc4	Rfe8
12.	Kg2	h6

65.

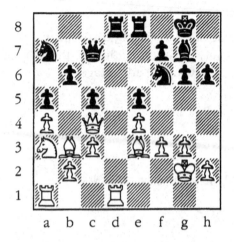

Having posted all his pieces (including his King) on good squares, White now has to tackle the problem of how to infiltrate. There is no obvious way to seize the open file, so he trades Rooks to create more free space.

13.	Rxd8	Rxd8
14.	Rd1	Rxd1
15.	Bxd1	Bf8
16.	Be2	Kg7
17.	Qb3	Ne8
18.	Ba6!	

The first hint of penetration. There is an immediate threat of 19. Nc4 winning the b Pawn (Black no longer has Nc8 as a defense), together with the long-term idea Qd5, Qa8, and Bb7 winning the Knight on a7.

18.	...	Nd6
19.	Qd5!	Ne8

He certainly cannot afford the further White-square weaknesses brought on by ...f6, e.g. 19...f6 20. Nc4 Nac8 (20...Nxc4? 21. Bxc4 and mates) 21. f4 exf4 22. Bxf4 with winning threats.

20. Nc4 Nf6

Losing a Pawn, but he has no good defense anyway. This time 20...f6 makes a spectacle exit viz. 21. Nxb6! Qxb6 22. Bc4 Qxb2+ 23. Kh3 with unstoppable mating threats. Objectively best is 20...Bd6, though he lacks a reply to 21 b4! axb4 22. cxb4, e.g. 22...cxb4 23. Bxb6 etc.

21. Qxe5 and White won.

In conclusion, a warning to those who would willingly accept a bad Bishop and a few weak squares in return for the slightest glimpse of an attack. As stressed earlier in the book, attacks must be built on the basis of a definite superiority in your position, either in development or in structure. To try to conjure up an attack out of thin air by artificial means is simply asking for trouble.

66.

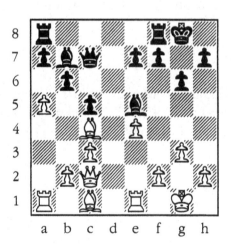

The position in Diagram 66 is dead equal, however, in the game Petrosian-Mecking, Palma 1969. Black (to move) allowed himself to be carried away by dreams of an attack:

1.	...	Bg7

Normal would be 1...Rfd8 with the bookmakers giving 3 to 1 on a draw.

2.	Bf4	e5?
3.	Bc1!	

Typical Petrosian. Bf4 was played with the sole intention of provoking the reply ...e5. Mission accomplished, he has no scruples about going back to square one. The Bishop maneuver has made two gains: (i) Black's King Bishop is becoming 'bad"; (ii) an outpost on d5. Moreover the Bishop retreat lures Black into a false sense of optimism about his attacking chances.

3.	...	Kh8
4.	Bd5	

Exchanging off Black's better Bishop.

4.	...	Bxd5
5.	exd5	f5

Black would be better advised to fix White's Queenside on Black squares by 5...c4, but he is still dreaming of winning a great victory on the Kingside.

6.	c4	Rae8
7.	Rd1	f4?

Taking one step too many in the wrong direction He must free his Bishop with 7...e4 when Black's prospects are still not too bad, e.g. 8. axb6 axb6 9. d6 Qc6 10. Ra7 Bd4! 11. Bf4 with chances for both sides, though maybe a few more for White than for Black.

8.	axb6	axb6
9.	Qe4!	

67.

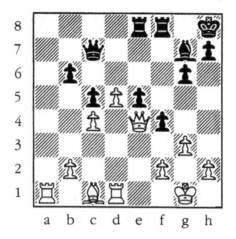

Compare Diagram 67 with Diagram 66. White has made all kings of positional gains: outpost on e4, good Bishop v. bad Bishop, protected passed Pawn etc. And Black? He has been telegraphing his intention to deliver mate for some time, but has grossly underestimated his opponent's defensive possibilities.

9.	...	Qd7
10.	Re1	

No need to panic. The secret of good defense is to keep calm and have faith in the inherent soundness of your position. In particular, don't be afraid of ghosts, i.e. don't make your opponent's threats out to be stronger than they actually are. For example, in this position, Black has two dangerous-looking plans: (i)...f3 and ...Qh3; (ii)...Qh3 and ...Rf5, Rh5 but a simple calculation reveals them to be innocuous:

(i) 10...f3 11. Ra3 brings the attack to an immediate halt, as Black must defend his Pawn.

(ii) 10...Qh3 11. Ra3 Rf5 12. Bxf4! Rh4 13. Qg2 and White has won a Pawn for nothing.

10. ...   **Qf7**

Now trying his hand on the f file, but again there is a simple defense.

11.   Re2

To meet ...fxg3 with hxg3 and there is no way in.

11. ...   **g5**
12.   g4!

Not only sealing up the Kingside, but also fixing yet another Pawn on a Black square.

12. ...   **Qd7**

Or 12...f3 13. Re1 h6 14. Ra3 and White can later round up the stray Pawn.

13.   f3

Completing his defensive program. We now see the difference between strategy and attack. Attacks can be repulsed, but positional advantages do not suddenly vanish without trace. Petrosian's quiet but logical play has left him with a stranglehold on the White squares which he will be able to exploit now that Black's threats have dried up.

13. ...   **Ra8**
14.   Rxa8 Rxa8
15.   Bd2

Stage one of the winning plan: tie Black's pieces to the defense of his e Pawn.

15.	...	Re8
16.	Bc3	Qd6
17.	Re1	

Stage two: switch to the a file.

17.	...	h6
18.	Ra1	Rf8
19.	Ra7	Re8
20.	Qf5	

Stage three: penetrate on the White squares. It couldn't be simpler.

20.	...	b5

Or 20...Rf8 21. Qd7 Qxd7 22. Rxd7 (threat Re7) Re8 23. Rb7 etc.

21.	Rd7	Qf8
22.	Qxf8+	Rxf8
23.	cxb5	Rb8??

A blunder in a hopeless situation.

24.	Rxg7	Black resigns (24...Kxg7 25. Bxe5+)

7. Space

The essence of simple chess is mobility. Pieces need to be kept active and used economically. All the objectives of simple chess can be traced back to this underlying notion. Outposts are springboards from which pieces can generate activity, weak Pawns hamper mobility because they require protection, 'bad' Bishops are bad because their movements are restricted. However, the single most important factor in determining mobility must be space, but what is space? Terms like 'White has the freer game', 'White has greater control', 'Black is cramped', crop up frequently in annotations, but what do they really mean and how is space apportioned?

Unlike the ideas expressed so far in this book, space is not an easily definable or recognizable concept. The visual impression you obtain by glancing at a position and estimating who seems to have the lion's share can be misleading. The following is nearer the truth. Any given Pawn structure has a certain capacity for accommodating pieces efficiently. Exceed this capacity and the pieces get in each other's way, and so reduce their mutual activity. This problem of overpopulation is easy to sense when playing a position—it 'feels' cramped. To take an example, compare Diagrams 68 and 69.

68.

69.

They do, of course, represent the same position, but with two pairs of minor pieces less in the second case. In Diagram 68 Black is terribly congested. There is no way he is ever going to be allowed to play ...b5, while alternative methods of seeking some breathing space by (after due preparation) ...e6 or ...f5 would compromise his Pawn structure considerably. White on the other hand can build up at leisure for an eventual e5, safe in the knowledge that so long as he avoids any piece exchange, his adversary will never be able to free his game. Diagram 69 is quite a contrast. The size of Black's forces is here well within his position's 'capacity'. As a result there are no spatial problems at all and Black can very quickly seize the initiative by ...a6 and ...b5, or even by ...b5 as a Pawn sacrifice, e.g. 1...b5 2. cxb5 a6 3. bxa6 Rxa6 with tremendous pressure. We see from this pair of positions that Black's structure is very good, but his capacity is small. Visually White has a spatial advantage in both cases, but in the second the eye flatters to deceive. In fact, he is grossly overextended. A vast empire requires an army of equal proportions to defend it.

Space is the most difficult element of chess strategy to understand. As we have just seen in Diagram 68, a position can be structurally very sound but actually very bad because of spatial problems. The real test of our insight into the mechanics of an advantage in space comes when confronted by a completely sound (structurally), solid but cramped position. How do you exploit such an advantage in space? Fischer provides all the answers.

White: R.J. Fischer, Black: F. Gheorghiu
Buenos Aires 1970

1. e4 e5 2. Nf3 Nf6 3. Nxe5 d6 4. Nf3 Nxe4 5. d4 Be7 (5...d5 is the standard move today. —*editor*) **6. Bd3 Nf6 7. h3! 0-0 8. 0-0 Re8 9. c4 Nc6 10. Nc3 h6**

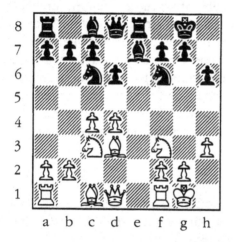

70

Black's position is very solid and devoid of weaknesses, yet he has some problem because his modest set-up is not equipped to hold a full complement of pieces. Put yourself in White's shoes and you might ask how you can possibly make any impression on the Black position, but that is the wrong approach. For the time being, White should maintain a low profile and concentrate on simple harmonious development, rather than which way he ought to be pointing his battering ram.

11.	Re1	Bf8

Naturally eager to swap off Rooks.

12.	Rxe8	Qxe8
13.	Bf4	Bd7
14.	Qd2	Qc8

There is no immediate danger, yet Black's position is uncomfortable. He wants to bring his Rook to e8 but is unable to do so because of his pieces are so constricted. For example, if 14...Qe7 (to prepare ...Re8), then 15. Re1 and the Queen must go back again. The only way to relieve the situation is by exchanges so Black prepares ...Bf5 to exchange Bishops, thus liberating the d7 square for his Queen which in turn allows the Rook a clear path to e8. For White's part it is sufficient to prevent this plan. When you have a spatial advantage there need be no hurry to form an active plan, that will come in due course. The important thing is to keep your opponent bottled up and put the onus on *him* to create active play. To do so he will be forced to weaken his own position somewhere. Only then do you pounce on him.

15.   d5

White would prefer to hold his Pawns on d4 and c4, but this advance in conjunction with Nd4 is the only way to prevent Black's freeing plan.

15.   ...   Nb4
16.   Ne4!

A neat finesse to preserve his King Bishop and gain time for Nd4, as the doubled Pawns after 16...Nxd3 17. Nxf6+ are naturally unacceptable for Black.

16.   ...   Nxe4
17.   Bxe4   Na6
18.   Nd4

71

Completing the hemming in maneuver. Now Black needs some fresh ideas. He can buy some space with 18...c5, but this saddles him with some sick Pawns after 19. dxc6 e.p bxc6. One of the main ideas in playing for space is that the opponent will some time 'trade off' his spatial inferiority for a structural one. Instead he elects to build an outpost on c5 for his Knight.

18.	...	Nc5
19.	Bc2	a5
20.	Re1	Qd8
21.	Re3!	

The King's file is itself of no use to White because he has no entry point, but it does enable him to put his Rook into active service on the third rank.

| 21. | ... | b6 |
| 22. | Rg3 | |

White's greater command of space now transforms itself into a concrete attack. The justifications for startling a direct offensive lies in the fact that Black's forces are concentrated on the Queenside and are unable to transfer across to aid the defense.

22.   ...   Kh8

The immediate threat was Bxh6.

23.   Nf3

Vacating the d4 square for the Queen. If Black seeks to anticipate this with 23...Qf6, there comes 24. Be3 and the Bishop takes up the lease on d4 with murderous effect.

23.   ...   Qe7
24.   Qd4

72.

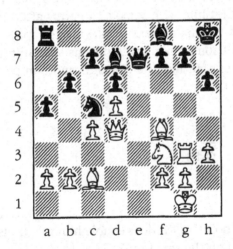

The culmination of White's play. Black's Kingside is raked by a crossfire of pins from which there is no shelter. Note that White is attacking with his entire army while Black is defending with but two pieces (Queen and Bishop), the rest being unable to communicate with the defense.

24.   ...   Qf6

138

The only defense to the threat of 25. Bxh6 (24...f6 25. Nh4 would be extremely gruesome).

25.   Qxf6   gxf6

Now it's back to Chapter 3. The weakness of the shattered Pawns is fatal. To begin with, White now has a juicy outpost on f5.

26.   Nd4   Re8
27.   Re3

Confident that his structural advantage is sufficient to win a minor piece ending. After 27...Rxe3 28. Bxe3 Kg7 29. Nf5+ Bxf5 30. Bxf5 the win is only a matter of time.

27.   ...   Rb8

Black shares his confidence. The remaining moves are desperation.

28.   b3   b5
29.   cxb5   Bxb5
30.   Nf5   Bd7

He can if he prefers to lose the Pawn on h4 vis. 30...h5 31. Ng3 h4 32. Nf5.

31.   Nxh6   Rb4
32.   Rg3!

With two separate mating threats.

32.   ...   Bxh6
33.   Bxh6   Ne4
34.   Bg7+   Kh7
35.   f3 and Black resigns.

So we see how easy it can be (or rather seem to be) to squeeze an opponent to death without any recourse to violence. The strategy behind playing to exploit a space advantage is twofold:

(i) Deprive the opponent of any counterplay, avoiding exchanges whenever possible. The psychological pressure of being permanently hemmed in may well induce him to weaken himself in order to gain some freedom.

(ii) If no weaknesses are forthcoming you must be prepared to attack on *either* wing. Greater space control gives you better communication between flanks, so you naturally want to exploit this fact to build up against the adversary's weaker front. In our last game, Fischer chose to attack on the Kingside because of the sparsity of Black forces in that region. Had the Black pieces been concentrated on the Kingside he would have resorted to a Queenside advance (b4 and c5). Flexibility of thought is needed to make use of flexibility on the board.

73.

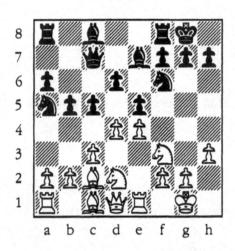

You have doubtless seen the move sequence: **1. e4 e5 2. Nf3 Nc6 3. Bb5 a6 4. Ba4 Nf6 5. 0-0 Be7 6. Re1 b5 7. Bb3 d6 8. c3 0-0 9. h3 Na5 10. Bc2 c5**

11. d4 Qc7 12. Nbd2 (Diagram 73) leading to the old main lines of the Ruy Lopez. Never in the history of chess have so many moves been repeated so often so quickly by so many people who didn't really understand them. Have you ever examined these well tried and trusted moves with a critical eye? Why, for example, should White spend twelve moves to develop just four pieces? Why waste four of these moves to preserve a Bishop which will in all probability later become 'bad' when White blocks the center with d5? By answering these questions, we can gain a lot of insight into White's overall strategy in the Lopez.

The first and most primitive idea behind 3. Bb5 is to lay seige to Black's e Pawn which will subsequently be liquidated by d4, thereby opening the floodgates for the White Pawn center to scatter the enemy forces with the allied pieces following up to rout the broken army—no prisoners taken. Black cannot however be forced to surrender the center. By keeping his own e Pawn firmly defended Black can thwart all White's aspirations of conquest in the center, but this will lead to a rather cramped position. So the offspring of White's plan is an advantage in space due to the necessity for his opponent to maintain a firm central barricade. This spatial plus however is not very big and the only way to maintain it is by avoiding any exchange of pieces. Black's position (Diagram 73) has sufficient 'capacity' for three minor pieces, but not clearly enough for all four of them. This explains why White is willing to invest so much time early in the game (Bb5, Ba4, Bb3, Bc2, h3) purely to avoid exchanges. If his spatial strategy is to succeed he must leave Black with four minor pieces. These closed Ruy Lopez positions are some of the most subtle and complex in the whole opening repertoire. It is probably no coincidence that nearly all the great players of recent times have been deadly exponents of the Ruy Lopez. In the hands of Fischer or Karpov 3. Bb5 sometimes appears to win by force. For example, Karpov-Westerinen, Nice 1974. **1. e4 e5 2. Nf3 Nc6 3. Bb5 a6 4. Ba4 d6 5. 0-0 Bd7 6. d4 Nf6 7. c3**

Be7 8. Nbd2 0-0 9. Re1 Re8 10. Nf1 h6 11. Ng3 Bf8

74.

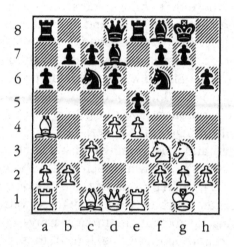

Here Black has adopted a less common form of defense. The idea is the same—to strongpoint his e5 Pawn.

12. Bd2

An unpretentious move, but White is not so much interested in promoting his own position as in containing his opponent's.

12. ... b5[?]

Better is 12...g6, depriving White of the f5 square. —*editor*

13. Bc2 Na5
14. b3 c5
15. d5!

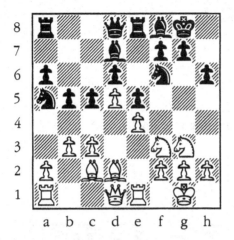

75

This in conjunction with his last move keeps the Knight on a5 firmly out of play. If now 15...c4, then 16. b4 Nb7 17. a4 gives White a clear structural advantage on the Queenside because he can open the a file at a time of *his* choosing, whereas Black can never resolve the position by ...bxa4 leaving himself with isolated Pawns everywhere.

15.	...	Nh7
16.	h3	

To meet ...Ng5 by Nh2 avoiding an exchange of Knights.

16.	...	Be7
17.	Nf5	

Confronting Black with a nasty dilemma. He needs to exchange some pieces to relieve his spatial problems, but ...Bxf5 gives up his best minor piece. Were he to take the Knight, he might well later fall victim to a White-square campaign, as his three central Pawns all stand on Black squares.

17.   ...   Nb7

By bolstering the defense of his d Pawn, Black now threatens to trade off his 'bad' Bishop with ...Bg5.

18.   a4   bxa4?

He clearly has not seen White's reply or he would have continued according to plan 18...Bg5 19. Nxg5 hxg5.

19.   b4!

76.

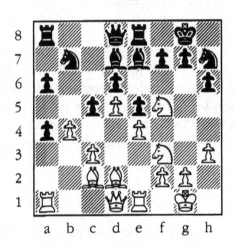

A surprise, but an entirely logical one. With this Pawn thrust he keeps the Black Knight bottled up on b7 while laying down the foundations for a positive strategy. By recapturing on a4 with his Bishop White can start to get to work on the White squares. For example, he suddenly acquires an outpost on c6. From the hazy depths of a purely spatial strategy we begin to see some concrete ideas emerging. It is very reasonable to assume that any position with an advantage in space will offer scope to translate the spatial plus into a structural one.

19.	...	a5

Black struggles hard to free himself by liquidating the Queenside, but the idea of opening up the position is fraught with danger as the Black pieces are much less mobile than their counterparts.

20.	Bxa4	axb4
21.	cxb4	Bf8

Changing plans in midstream is bound to be fatal, but so is the logical complement of Black's play 21...cxb4 on account of 22. Bxd7 and now:

(i) 22...Qxd7 allows the bolt from the blue 23. Nxe5, as after 23...dxe5 24. Qg4 the double threat of mate and Nxh6+ will cost Black his Queen, while 23...Rxa1 24. Qg4! Rxe1+ 25. Bxe1 has similar effect.

(ii) 22...Rxa1 23. Qxa1 Qxd7 24. Bxb4 leaves Black powerless to prevent White's Queen penetrating on the a file, e.g. 24...Qb5? 25. Nxe5 (again!) Qxb4 (or 25...dxe5 26. Nxe7+) 26. Nc6 threatening mate on g7 as well as the Queen and Bishop.

22.	Bc6!

Now Black is smothered. He cannot trade Bishops because the Knight on b7 would then have nowhere to go, so he must allow the establishment of a protected passed Bishop in the midst of his Queenside encampment.

22.	...	Qc7
23.	b5	Nf6

Black's moves from this juncture are, essentially, irrelevant. There is no way he can in the long run hope to hold his Queenside position, which has the look of Custer's last stand about it. Although he has only one vulnerable Pawn (d6), Black's pieces are so starved of space that they

145

are themselves becoming targets of attack. After all, we only normally choose to attack Pawns because of their inability to run away, but when the pieces themselves have no escape squares why not go in search of bigger game?

24.	Qc2	Reb8
25.	Ne3	Bc8
26.	Nc4	Be7
27.	b6	Qd8
28.	Ra7	

77.

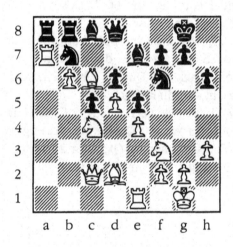

Making use of his latest acquisition, an outpost on a7! It is now only a matter of time before Black is pushed off the edge of the board.

28.	...	Nd7
29.	Qa4	Rxa7
30.	bxa7	Ra8
31.	Qa6	Qc7
32.	Bxd7	

Winning by force. The entry of the White Knight on b6 is decisive.

32.	...	Qxd7

Or 32...Bxd7 33. Nb6 winning at least a Rook.

33.	Nb6	Nd8
34.	Qa1!	

Very artistic. If now 34...Qxa7 35. Qxa7 and 36. Nxc8, or 34...Rxa7 35. Nxd7 Rxa1 36. Rxa1 Bxd7 37. Ra7 winning some more, so Black resigned.

Undoubtedly the most difficult game in the book to understand. One can only really begin to appreciate the idea of converting spatial advantages into structural ones when the latter have been fully absorbed and understood. The closed Ruy Lopez positions represent a very fine balance between space and structure which only becomes apparent after many years of experience with them. When you understand the Lopez, you have mastered simple chess.

Our brief excursion into the Ruy Lopez has scratched the surface of some of the deeper aspects of chess strategy, but we will proceed no further in this direction. The idea of this book is to keep things simple, so let us look at some of the more direct consequences of spatial advantages. Space, or lack of it, is generally used as a way of persuading the opponent to make structural concessions. Let us take for example a (quite common) Pawn structure, Diagram 78.

78.

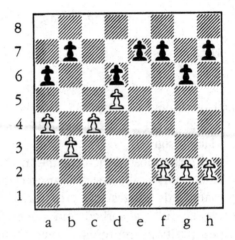

Black's set-up is very sound but its 'capacity' is low, so given a position with some major pieces and a few minor pieces each, he would have some spatial problems. Structurally speaking he has two ways to combat them:

(i) Undermine White's center by ...b5. This is the positionally correct method, but is in practice often difficult to organize as White can usually keep quite a strong grip on the b5 square (with, say, Knight on d4, c3, Bishop on f1-a6 diagonal). An added problem is that moving the b Pawn gives White an outpost on c6 for his Knight.

(ii) Challenge White's Pawn wedge by ...e6. But this creates structural weaknesses. The Black d Pawn is left very weak after White exchanges Pawns on e6 and the Black Kingside is also weakened somewhat.

Practice has shown that Pawn structure akin to Diagram 78 are very favorable for White providing that Black's minority attack ...b5 can be prevented. In this case the exploitation of White's spatial advantage is not all difficult to understand. He can utilize his greater control and communication between wings to launch a direct Kingside attack.

White: L. Portisch, Black: S. Reshevsky
Petropolis 1973

1. c4 c5 2. Nf3 g6 3. e4 Nc6 4. d4 cxd4 5. Nxd4
Nf6 6. Nc3 Nxd4 7. Qxd4 d6 8. Bg5 Bg7 9. Qd2
0-0 10. Bd3

79.

We do not yet have the Pawn structure of Diagram 78,
but White can some day plant his Knight on d5, and recapture
with the e Pawn when Black takes it off. Of course, the whole
plan can be prevented by Black playing ...e6 at almost any
stage, but this would leave him with a very sick d Pawn on an
open file. Simple chess always requires flexibility of thought.
The opponent can always avert one form of weaknesses or
disadvantage by accepting another somewhere else.

10   ...   a5

Acknowledging from the start that he will never be
permitted to play ...b5, since after the natural plan of
10...Rb8 and 11...Bd7 there comes a4 by White and that's the
end of that. Instead, Black aims to steal some space on the
Queenside to offset his lack of it in the center.

11.	0-0	a4
12.	Rac1	

To keep Black guessing. White could be intending to play Nd5 and recapture with the c Pawn. You never can tell—

12.	...	Be6
13.	Qc2	

He can of course play Nd5 immediately, as after 13...Nxd5 14. exd5 Bd7 15. Rfe1 White stands better, but Nd5 can never be prevented so why not probe a little first?

13.	...	Nd7

An indirect defense of the a Pawn (14. Nxa4? Qa5 hitting two pieces). The natural 13...Qa5 would make 14. Nd5 correspondingly stronger:

(i) 14...Nxd5 15. exd5 and Black's e Pawn is hanging.

(ii) 14...Bxd5 15. cxd5 (you never could tell!) and White controls the c file with an entry point on c7.

14.	f4

A signal of the impending Kingside attack. For the moment the threat is f5 winning the Bishop.

14.	...	Rc8
15.	b3	axb3
16.	axb3	Nf6

Very passive, but alternatives are hardly more palatable:

(i) 16...Nc5 17. f5 Nxd3 18. Qxd3 Bd7 19. Nd5 leaves Black in terrible trouble (19...Re8 20. f6!).

(ii) 16... f5 17. Rce1 and the pressure on the e file is felt right the way back to Black's e Pawn.

17.	Kh1	Qa5
18.	f5	Bd7
19.	Nd5!	

80.

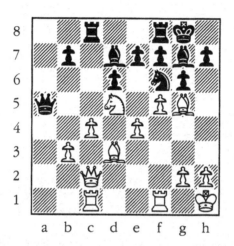

The moment we've all been waiting for. After 19...Nxd5 20. exd5, White has through his spatial advantage very good attacking chances against the Black King, e.g. 20...Rfe8 21. Rce1 Qd8 22. fxg6 hxg6 23. Bxg6! fxg6 24. Qxg6 Rf8 25. Bh6 forcing mate.

19.	...	Qd8!

A good defensive try, in that 20. Nxf6+ Bxf6 21. Bxf6 exf6 leads nowhere for White as he is left with a bad Bishop and many Black-square weaknesses. The correct way to pursue the attack is by increasing the pressure without permitting too much simplification.

20.	Qf2	Bc6
21.	Qh4	Bxd5

The presence of the Knight on d5 has eventually proved too much for Black to tolerate, but now White obtains the Pawn formation he has been seeking all along.

151

22.	exd5	Re8
23.	Rf3	Nd7
24.	Rcf1	Bf6

Black would like to establish his Knight on the outpost at e5, but then there would come 24...Ne5 25. Rh3 h5 26. fxg6 fxg6 27. Bxg6! Nxg6 28. Qxh5 Nf8 29. Qf7 mate. Instead he hopes to trade Bishops and erect a defense on the Black squares, but in doing so he is destroyed by a combination.

25.	Rh3	Nf8
26.	fxg6	fxg6
27.	Bxg6!	hxg6
28.	Rxf6!	

and Black resigned as it is mate after **28...exf6 29. Qh8+ Kf7 30. Rh7+ Nxh7 31. Qxh7+ Kf8 32. Bh6** mate.

Another game in which correct nursing of a spatial plus results in a direct attack:

White: V. Smyslov, Black: K. Gudmundsson
Reykjavik 1974

1. d4 Nf6 2. Nf3 g6 3. b3 Bg7 4. Bb2 0-0 5. g3 d6 6. Bg2 c5 7. 0-0 Nc6 8. d5 Na5 9. c4 a6 10. Nbd2 b5 11. e4 Rb8 12. Bc3 Qc7 13. e5 Ng4 14. exd6 exd6 15. Bxg7 Kxg7

81.

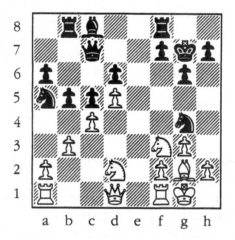

It is immediately obvious that White has more space because of his Pawn wedge on d5, but Black has obtained an aggressive set-up on the Queenside by ...b5. Indeed, one might even venture to say that Black has a slight structural superiority because he has some pressure on the base of White's Pawn center (c4) and first option on the b file, whereas the counterpressure against the base of Black's center (d6) is not evident. Once again the trouble with Black's position is with communications. His Queenside position is a favorable one, but lacks contact with the rest of the war effort. If White can successfully conduct a holding operation on the Queenside, some of Black's pieces (particularly the Knight on a5) will be left very much out of play.

16. Re1   f6

To increase the pressure on White's c Pawn by establishing a Knight on e5. In the event of an exchange there, Black wants to recapture with the f Pawn. The immediate 16...Ne5 17. Nxe5 dxe5 not only gives his adversary a strong passed Pawn, but also weakens his own c Pawn, e.g. 18. Rc1 threatening 19. cxb5 axb5 20. b4!

17.   Qc1

Sounder than Qc2 which might some time allow an embarrassing ...Bf5. Besides, with his central Pawn configuration on White squares he would prefer his Queen on a Black square as a matter of principle.

17.   ...   Ne5
18.   Bf1

Completing his consolidation of the Queenside. For the moment White's position looks to be the more passive, as indeed it is. But at this point the spatial consideration begins to take over. Black's position has already almost reached its peak. He has no capacity to expand or exert more pressure without creating weaknesses in his own camp. On the other hand, the White forces although temporarily at a low ebb, have plenty of opportunity to drive forward in the longer term because of the greater space potentially available to them.

18.   ...   Bg4

In essence the right idea—Black would like to force some exchanges—but his mission turns out to be singularly unsuccessful. He would do better to trade Knights while he still has the chance, e.g. 18...Nxf3+ 19. Nxf3 bxc4 20. bxc4 Rb4 possibly followed by the maneuver Nb7, Nd8 Nf7, Ne5. Black is willing to expend a great deal of time and energy to provoke the exchange of the second pair of Knights. His position is fundamentally quite sound, but simply lacking in space.

19.   Nh4!

Very instructive. White wants to avoid exchanges, so any old square will do for the Knight as long as all the pieces stay on.

154

19.	...	bxc4
20.	bxc4	Rfe8
21.	f4	

The great wheel of fortune begins to turn in White's favor. As he expands his own position the Black pieces will start to tread on each other's toes for lack of space.

| 21. | ... | Nf7 |

d7 would be a better square for the Knight, but this would excommunicate the Bishop (22. h3 etc.).

| 22. | Qc3 | |

The threat to win a Pawn by 23. Ne4 Qd8 24. Nxf6 Qxf6 25.Qxa5 now induces a full-scale retreat.

22.	...	Rxe1
23.	Rxe1	Nb7
24.	h3	Bd7
25.	Ne4	Qd8
26.	g4!	

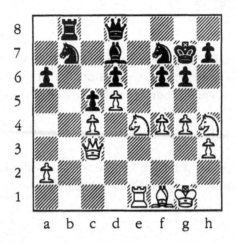

82

Compare this with White's modest position some ten moves ago. His conquest of space has brought him a decisive Kingside attack (the threat of g5 is unstoppable) almost as an incidental by-product.

```
26.  ...   h6
27.  Bd3
```

Smyslov chooses the most elegant method. Naturally the cruder 27. g5 is also very strong.

```
27.  ...   g5
28.  Ng3!
```

The point of his previous move. White can give up a piece for a mating attack. The subsequent helplessness of the Black forces is quite remarkable.

```
28.  ...   gxh4
29.  Nh5+  Kf8
30.  Nxf6  Ba4
```

What else? There is nothing to be done against 31. Nh5 and 32. Qg7 mate.

31. Nh5 Ne5

32. fxe5 and Black resigned.

Playing on the basis of a spatial advantage is in a sense a question of blind faith. You see no targets in the enemy position and no way to force any weaknesses, but merely attempt to fortify your own position allowing simplification only when absolutely necessary or clearly favorable in the belief that your opponent will some time feel obliged to make concrete concessions in terms of Pawn weaknesses or outposts in order to avoid suffocation. The difficult part of a spatial strategy lies not in the execution which is relatively simple, but in the recognition of the fact that you actually do have an advantage in space. As already mentioned, the vital criterion is not necessarily whether you 'appear' to control more of the board. This is undoubtedly a yardstick, but not always an accurate one. The real criterion is whether your opponent has more pieces than can comfortably fit in with his Pawn structure, and this you can only really expect to assess correctly on the basis of experience. From your own games and by studying master games you can gradually acquire a feeling for the 'capacity' (as I earlier termed it) of certain Pawn structures. Space is not an easy concept to define with precision or understand with clarity, but time and practice will sharpen your awareness of it as a factor in chess. I have tried throughout the book to lay down principles and put forward ideas that relate to all phases of the game, opening, middlegame, and endgame, and space is no exception. The role played by space in the endgame is in fact much more straightforward than in the middlegame. In the endings the King assumes greater power and, consequently, value. The advantage of being first to occupy the center with your King is considerable. He who commands more space has more squares for his King, it's as simple as that. More space means a potentially stronger King.

White: T. Petrosian, Black: L. Portisch
Candidate's Match (5th Game) 1974

1. c4 Nf6 2. Nf3 b6 3. g3 c5 4. Bg2 Bg7 5. 0-0 e6
6. Nc3 Be7 7. d4 cxd4 8. Qxd4 0-0 9. Rd1 Nc6 10. Qf4
Qb8 11. e4(!) Qxf4 12. Bxf4 Rfd8 13. e5 Ne8
14. Nd4 Na5 15. b3 Bxg2 16. Kxg2 g5?! 17. Be3 Kg7

83.

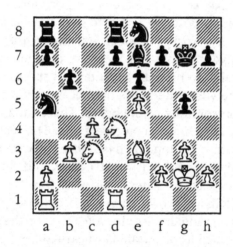

White has more space on account of his advanced
Pawn on e5 which in turn gives him a very good square on e4
for his King, while Black through lack of space has no central
squares available for his own leader.

18. f4

A surprising move in that White voluntarily places his
Pawns on squares of the same color as his Bishop, but
Petrosian reckons his grip on the center to be more
important.

18.	...	gxf4
19.	gxf4	Nc6
20.	Nce2	

Against the natural 20. Kf3 there comes 20...f5 barring the White King from e4, but now 20...f5 can be met by 21. Nxc6 dxc6 22. Nd4 winning a Pawn.

20.   ...   Nxd4
21.   Nxd4 Bc5

Continuing with his policy of exchanges. If 21...Rac8 White has the strong continuation 22. Nb5 a6 23. Bxb6! axb5 24. Bxd8 Rxd8 25. cxb5 netting a Rook and an impressive array of passed Pawns for two pieces.

22.   Kf3   d6
23.   Rd2!

A remarkably strong move after which the Black King suddenly finds himself in trouble. He could of course abdicate his responsibilities and seek refuge on some godforsaken edge of the board where he would be relatively safe, but then the rest of the position would crumble through lack of his support. For example, White threatens Rad1 followed by Nb5 with decisive threats on the d file. Black's only chance of survival is to bring his King into the center to bolster his defenses.

23.   ...   dxe5
24.   fxe5   Bxd4

Again Portisch seeks to relieve his position by exchanges, but this still does not help his King to find a satisfactory square in the center.

25.   Bxd4   f6

Desperation, but if 25...Kf8, then 26. Rad1 leaves Black defenseless viz.
(i) 26...Ke7 27. c5 Rab8 (27...b5 28. c6!) 28. cxb6 axb6 29. Bxb6! Rxd2 30. Bc5+.

159

(ii) 26...Ng7 (or c7) 27. Bxb6! Rxd2 28. Bc5!.
(iii) 26...Rdc8 27. Be3 followed by Bh6+ etc.

26.   exf6+ Nxf6
27.   Rf1

Threatening to win a piece by 28. Ke3.

27.   ...   Kh6
28.   Re1

Winning the e Pawn as 28...Re8 unpins the Bishop
allowing 29. Bxf6, while 28...Rd6 loses to 29. Be3+. The rest is
very one-sided: **28...Ng8 29. Rxe6+ Kh5 30. Re5+ Kg6
31. Rg2+ Kf7 32. Re4 Nf6 33. Rf4 Rd6 34. Rg5
Rad8 35. Rd5!** Black resigns (For if 35...Rxd5 36. Rxf6+ Ke7
37. cxd5 Rxd5 38. Rf4).

A CATALOG OF SELECTED
DOVER BOOKS
IN ALL FIELDS OF INTEREST

A CATALOG OF SELECTED DOVER
BOOKS IN ALL FIELDS OF INTEREST

CONCERNING THE SPIRITUAL IN ART, Wassily Kandinsky. Pioneering work by father of abstract art. Thoughts on color theory, nature of art. Analysis of earlier masters. 12 illustrations. 80pp. of text. 5⅜ x 8¼.　　　　0-486-23411-8

CELTIC ART: The Methods of Construction, George Bain. Simple geometric techniques for making Celtic interlacements, spirals, Kells-type initials, animals, humans, etc. Over 500 illustrations. 160pp. 9 x 12. (Available in U.S. only.)　　　　0-486-22923-8

AN ATLAS OF ANATOMY FOR ARTISTS, Fritz Schider. Most thorough reference work on art anatomy in the world. Hundreds of illustrations, including selections from works by Vesalius, Leonardo, Goya, Ingres, Michelangelo, others. 593 illustrations. 192pp. 7⅛ x 10¼.　　　　0-486-20241-0

CELTIC HAND STROKE-BY-STROKE (Irish Half-Uncial from "The Book of Kells"): An Arthur Baker Calligraphy Manual, Arthur Baker. Complete guide to creating each letter of the alphabet in distinctive Celtic manner. Covers hand position, strokes, pens, inks, paper, more. Illustrated. 48pp. 8¼ x 11.　　　　0-486-24336-2

EASY ORIGAMI, John Montroll. Charming collection of 32 projects (hat, cup, pelican, piano, swan, many more) specially designed for the novice origami hobbyist. Clearly illustrated easy-to-follow instructions insure that even beginning papercrafters will achieve successful results. 48pp. 8¼ x 11.　　　　0-486-27298-2

BLOOMINGDALE'S ILLUSTRATED 1886 CATALOG: Fashions, Dry Goods and Housewares, Bloomingdale Brothers. Famed merchants' extremely rare catalog depicting about 1,700 products: clothing, housewares, firearms, dry goods, jewelry, more. Invaluable for dating, identifying vintage items. Also, copyright-free graphics for artists, designers. Co-published with Henry Ford Museum & Greenfield Village. 160pp. 8¼ x 11.　　　　0-486-25780-0

THE ART OF WORLDLY WISDOM, Baltasar Gracian. "Think with the few and speak with the many," "Friends are a second existence," and "Be able to forget" are among this 1637 volume's 300 pithy maxims. A perfect source of mental and spiritual refreshment, it can be opened at random and appreciated either in brief or at length. 128pp. 5⅜ x 8½.　　　　0-486-44034-6

JOHNSON'S DICTIONARY: A Modern Selection, Samuel Johnson (E. L. McAdam and George Milne, eds.). This modern version reduces the original 1755 edition's 2,300 pages of definitions and literary examples to a more manageable length, retaining the verbal pleasure and historical curiosity of the original. 480pp. 5³⁄₁₆ x 8¼.　　　　0-486-44089-3

ADVENTURES OF HUCKLEBERRY FINN, Mark Twain, Illustrated by E. W. Kemble. A work of eternal richness and complexity, a source of ongoing critical debate, and a literary landmark, Twain's 1885 masterpiece about a barefoot boy's journey of self-discovery has enthralled readers around the world. This handsome clothbound reproduction of the first edition features all 174 of the original black-and-white illustrations. 368pp. 5⅜ x 8½.　　　　0-486-44322-1

STICKLEY CRAFTSMAN FURNITURE CATALOGS, Gustav Stickley and L. & J. G. Stickley. Beautiful, functional furniture in two authentic catalogs from 1910. 594 illustrations, including 277 photos, show settles, rockers, armchairs, reclining chairs, bookcases, desks, tables. 183pp. 6½ x 9¼. 0-486-23838-5

AMERICAN LOCOMOTIVES IN HISTORIC PHOTOGRAPHS: 1858 to 1949, Ron Ziel (ed.). A rare collection of 126 meticulously detailed official photographs, called "builder portraits," of American locomotives that majestically chronicle the rise of steam locomotive power in America. Introduction. Detailed captions. xi+ 129pp. 9 x 12. 0-486-27393-8

AMERICA'S LIGHTHOUSES: An Illustrated History, Francis Ross Holland, Jr. Delightfully written, profusely illustrated fact-filled survey of over 200 American light-houses since 1716. History, anecdotes, technological advances, more. 240pp. 8 x 10¾. 0-486-25576-X

TOWARDS A NEW ARCHITECTURE, Le Corbusier. Pioneering manifesto by founder of "International School." Technical and aesthetic theories, views of industry, eco-nomics, relation of form to function, "mass-production split" and much more. Profusely illustrated. 320pp. 6⅛ x 9¼. (Available in U.S. only.) 0-486-25023-7

HOW THE OTHER HALF LIVES, Jacob Riis. Famous journalistic record, expos-ing poverty and degradation of New York slums around 1900, by major social reformer. 100 striking and influential photographs. 233pp. 10 x 7⅞. 0-486-22012-5

FRUIT KEY AND TWIG KEY TO TREES AND SHRUBS, William M. Harlow. One of the handiest and most widely used identification aids. Fruit key covers 120 deciduous and evergreen species; twig key 160 deciduous species. Easily used. Over 300 photographs. 126pp. 5⅜ x 8½. 0-486-20511-8

COMMON BIRD SONGS, Dr. Donald J. Borror. Songs of 60 most common U.S. birds: robins, sparrows, cardinals, bluejays, finches, more—arranged in order of increasing complexity. Up to 9 variations of songs of each species. Cassette and manual 0-486-99911-4

ORCHIDS AS HOUSE PLANTS, Rebecca Tyson Northen. Grow cattleyas and many other kinds of orchids—in a window, in a case, or under artificial light. 63 illus-trations. 148pp. 5⅜ x 8½. 0-486-23261-1

MONSTER MAZES, Dave Phillips. Masterful mazes at four levels of difficulty. Avoid deadly perils and evil creatures to find magical treasures. Solutions for all 32 exciting illustrated puzzles. 48pp. 8¼ x 11. 0-486-26005-4

MOZART'S DON GIOVANNI (DOVER OPERA LIBRETTO SERIES), Wolfgang Amadeus Mozart. Introduced and translated by Ellen H. Bleiler. Standard Italian libretto, with complete English translation. Convenient and thoroughly portable—an ideal companion for reading along with a recording or the performance itself. Introduction. List of characters. Plot summary. 121pp. 5¼ x 8½. 0-486-24944-1

FRANK LLOYD WRIGHT'S DANA HOUSE, Donald Hoffmann. Pictorial essay of residential masterpiece with over 160 interior and exterior photos, plans, eleva-tions, sketches and studies. 128pp. 9¹/₄ x 10¾. 0-486-29120-0

HINTS TO SINGERS, Lillian Nordica. Selecting the right teacher, developing confidence, overcoming stage fright, and many other important skills receive thoughtful discussion in this indispensible guide, written by a world-famous diva of four decades' experience. 96pp. 5⅜ x 8½. 0-486-40094-8

THE COMPLETE NONSENSE OF EDWARD LEAR, Edward Lear. All nonsense limericks, zany alphabets, Owl and Pussycat, songs, nonsense botany, etc., illustrated by Lear. Total of 320pp. 5⅜ x 8½. (Available in U.S. only.) 0-486-20167-8

VICTORIAN PARLOUR POETRY: An Annotated Anthology, Michael R. Turner. 117 gems by Longfellow, Tennyson, Browning, many lesser-known poets. "The Village Blacksmith," "Curfew Must Not Ring Tonight," "Only a Baby Small," dozens more, often difficult to find elsewhere. Index of poets, titles, first lines. xxiii + 325pp. 5⅝ x 8¼. 0-486-27044-0

DUBLINERS, James Joyce. Fifteen stories offer vivid, tightly focused observations of the lives of Dublin's poorer classes. At least one, "The Dead," is considered a masterpiece. Reprinted complete and unabridged from standard edition. 160pp. 5³⁄₁₆ x 8¼. 0-486-26870-5

GREAT WEIRD TALES: 14 Stories by Lovecraft, Blackwood, Machen and Others, S. T. Joshi (ed.). 14 spellbinding tales, including "The Sin Eater," by Fiona McLeod, "The Eye Above the Mantel," by Frank Belknap Long, as well as renowned works by R. H. Barlow, Lord Dunsany, Arthur Machen, W. C. Morrow and eight other masters of the genre. 256pp. 5⅜ x 8½. (Available in U.S. only.) 0-486-40436-6

THE BOOK OF THE SACRED MAGIC OF ABRAMELIN THE MAGE, translated by S. MacGregor Mathers. Medieval manuscript of ceremonial magic. Basic document in Aleister Crowley, Golden Dawn groups. 268pp. 5⅜ x 8½. 0-486-23211-5

THE BATTLES THAT CHANGED HISTORY, Fletcher Pratt. Eminent historian profiles 16 crucial conflicts, ancient to modern, that changed the course of civilization. 352pp. 5⅜ x 8½. 0-486-41129-X

NEW RUSSIAN-ENGLISH AND ENGLISH-RUSSIAN DICTIONARY, M. A. O'Brien. This is a remarkably handy Russian dictionary, containing a surprising amount of information, including over 70,000 entries. 366pp. 4½ x 6⅛. 0-486-20208-9

NEW YORK IN THE FORTIES, Andreas Feininger. 162 brilliant photographs by the well-known photographer, formerly with *Life* magazine. Commuters, shoppers, Times Square at night, much else from city at its peak. Captions by John von Hartz. 181pp. 9¼ x 10¾. 0-486-23585-8

INDIAN SIGN LANGUAGE, William Tomkins. Over 525 signs developed by Sioux and other tribes. Written instructions and diagrams. Also 290 pictographs. 111pp. 6⅛ x 9¼. 0-486-22029-X

ANATOMY: A Complete Guide for Artists, Joseph Sheppard. A master of figure drawing shows artists how to render human anatomy convincingly. Over 460 illustrations. 224pp. 8⅜ x 11¼. 0-486-27279-6

MEDIEVAL CALLIGRAPHY: Its History and Technique, Marc Drogin. Spirited history, comprehensive instruction manual covers 13 styles (ca. 4th century through 15th). Excellent photographs; directions for duplicating medieval techniques with modern tools. 224pp. 8⅜ x 11¼. 0-486-26142-5

LIGHT AND SHADE: A Classic Approach to Three-Dimensional Drawing, Mrs. Mary P. Merrifield. Handy reference clearly demonstrates principles of light and shade by revealing effects of common daylight, sunshine, and candle or artificial light on geometrical solids. 13 plates. 64pp. 5⅜ x 8½. 0-486-44143-1

ASTROLOGY AND ASTRONOMY: A Pictorial Archive of Signs and Symbols, Ernst and Johanna Lehner. Treasure trove of stories, lore, and myth, accompanied by more than 300 rare illustrations of planets, the Milky Way, signs of the zodiac, comets, meteors, and other astronomical phenomena. 192pp. 8⅜ x 11.
0-486-43981-X

JEWELRY MAKING: Techniques for Metal, Tim McCreight. Easy-to-follow instructions and carefully executed illustrations describe tools and techniques, use of gems and enamels, wire inlay, casting, and other topics. 72 line illustrations and diagrams. 176pp. 8¼ x 10⅞. 0-486-44043-5

MAKING BIRDHOUSES: Easy and Advanced Projects, Gladstone Califf. Easy-to-follow instructions include diagrams for everything from a one-room house for blue-birds to a forty-two-room structure for purple martins. 56 plates; 4 figures. 80pp. 8¾ x 6⅜. 0-486-44183-0

LITTLE BOOK OF LOG CABINS: How to Build and Furnish Them, William S. Wicks. Handy how-to manual, with instructions and illustrations for building cabins in the Adirondack style, fireplaces, stairways, furniture, beamed ceilings, and more. 102 line drawings. 96pp. 8¾ x 6⅜. 0-486-44259-4

THE SEASONS OF AMERICA PAST, Eric Sloane. From "sugaring time" and strawberry picking to Indian summer and fall harvest, a whole year's activities described in charming prose and enhanced with 79 of the author's own illustrations. 160pp. 8¼ x 11. 0-486-44220-9

THE METROPOLIS OF TOMORROW, Hugh Ferriss. Generous, prophetic vision of the metropolis of the future, as perceived in 1929. Powerful illustrations of towering structures, wide avenues, and rooftop parks—all features in many of today's modern cities. 59 illustrations. 144pp. 8¼ x 11. 0-486-43727-2

THE PATH TO ROME, Hilaire Belloc. This 1902 memoir abounds in lively vignettes from a vanished time, recounting a pilgrimage on foot across the Alps and Apennines in order to "see all Europe which the Christian Faith has saved." 77 of the author's original line drawings complement his sparkling prose. 272pp. 5⅜ x 8½.
0-486-44001-X

THE HISTORY OF RASSELAS: Prince of Abissinia, Samuel Johnson. Distinguished English writer attacks eighteenth-century optimism and man's unrealistic estimates of what life has to offer. 112pp. 5⅜ x 8½. 0-486-44094-X

A VOYAGE TO ARCTURUS, David Lindsay. A brilliant flight of pure fancy, where wild creatures crowd the fantastic landscape and demented torturers dominate victims with their bizarre mental powers. 272pp. 5⅜ x 8½. 0-486-44198-9

Paperbound unless otherwise indicated. Available at your book dealer, online at **www.doverpublications.com**, or by writing to Dept. GI, Dover Publications, Inc., 31 East 2nd Street, Mineola, NY 11501. For current price information or for free catalogs (please indicate field of interest), write to Dover Publications or log on to **www.doverpublications.com** and see every Dover book in print. Dover publishes more than 500 books each year on science, elementary and advanced mathematics, biology, music, art, literary history, social sciences, and other areas.